the 5-ingredient
keto cookbook

the 5-ingredient

keto cookbook

100 Easy Ketogenic
Recipes

STEPHANIE PEDERSEN

AUTHOR OF *Keto Lunches* AND *The Keto Kit*

STERLING EPICURE
New York

STERLING EPICURE
New York

An Imprint of Sterling Publishing Co., Inc.
1166 Avenue of the Americas
New York, NY 10036

ISBN 978-1-4549-4021-0

Distributed in Canada by Sterling Publishing Co., Inc.
C/o Canadian Manda Group, 664 Annette Street
Toronto, Ontario M6S 2C8, Canada
Distributed in the United Kingdom by GMC Distribution Services
Castle Place, 166 High Street, Lewes, East Sussex BN7 1XU, England
Distributed in Australia by NewSouth Books
University of New South Wales, Sydney, NSW 2052, Australia

For information about custom editions, special sales, and premium
and corporate purchases, please contact Sterling Special Sales
at 800-805-5489 or specialsales@sterlingpublishing.com.

Manufactured in Spain

2 4 6 8 10 9 7 5 3 1

sterlingpublishing.com

Cover design by David Ter-Avanesyan
Interior Design by Christine Heun

Photo Credits

COVER:
Stocksy: © Nadine Greeff

INTERIOR:
Getty Images: Bartosz Luczak 37, LUMIKK555 (blue background throughout),
Pamela D. Mcadams 52, Olga Miltsova xi, Mustafahacalaki 3, Nastco (black
background throughout), Roxiller 4, Anamaria Tegzes 11, Sveta Zarzamora xi

Bill Milne: 19, 22, 47, 50, 55, 67, 73, 81, 86, 93, 109, 114, 120, 129, 132, 136

Stockfood: © Petr Gross 62

Stocksy: © Dobránska Renáta 29

© Alyssa Peek: 163

*

I dedicate this book to you,
dear reader. Be you a die-hard
keto eater or a high-fat newbie,
happy meal making. May
you find what you need in
the pages of this book.

*

Avocado, shrimp, spiralized zucchini, and greens (with or without a sprinkling of parmesan) make an easy, free-form meal. No recipe needed!

Contents

Introduction

THERE IS NO DENYING THAT THE keto diet is one of the most-talked-about eating plans around. Thousands of books, blogs, websites, podcasts, snack foods, expos, and other resources exist, all dedicated to ketogenic eating. And yet, despite the enormous amount of keto information out there, one thing remains true: Finding food to eat on the keto diet can be difficult. Although it's true that hundreds of niche companies have rushed in to serve the keto market, you can't live on packaged food!

That's where *The 5-Ingredient Keto Cookbook* comes in. Whether you've been on the low-carb, high-fat eating journey for a while now, or are just dipping your toe into the world of macro counting, you have most likely noticed how fiddly and complicated keto recipes can be—and how long their ingredient lists are!

Here's the reason why: When using low-carb ingredients to mimic traditional-style carbohydrate-rich dishes, you need a few work-arounds to approximate the delicious flavors and textures of the mainstream meals you love. What's more, keto cooking is about healthy fats—extraordinarily generous amounts of healthy fats. Cooking with so much fat requires a bit more finesse than simply sneaking a few extra tablespoons of mashed avocado or coconut oil into your favorite recipe.

At this point, you may be tempted to pick up the phone and order keto takeout or dive into the world of premade delivery meals. Those are fine options, but no matter what diet you are following (or not following) or what foods you choose to enjoy, learning how to make your own meals—knowing exactly what is going into each dish you put on the table—is the healthiest, most effective way to literally watch what you eat.

That's what *The 5-Ingredient Keto Cookbook* is all about: showing you how to prepare easy-to-make keto-compliant meals with familiar ingredients that you probably already have in your own kitchen—or can find at your local grocery store.

And that's not all. To keep your eating plan on track, all recipes in *The 5-Ingredient Keto Cookbook* contain macro counts, so you know how to plan your meals and food intake every day.

In chapter 1, Keto Eating and How to Use this Cookbook, you'll get the lowdown on the ketogenic diet, including the science behind the eating plan, some of its quirks, and what changes you can expect to see in your body. This is the book's foundational chapter, and it's where you'll learn how to get the most out of *The 5-Ingredient Keto Cookbook.*

One of the most overlooked—and important—ways to ensure keto success is to set up your kitchen in a way that makes keto cooking a snap. That's why *The 5-Ingredient Keto Cookbook* includes a comprehensive education in outfitting and organizing a keto-friendly pantry and kitchen,

Chapter 2, Setting Up Your Pantry, covers everything a new keto cook needs to know, from giving you the lowdown on what ingredients to purchase (and how to use and store them) to the kitchen gadgets that no keto home cook should be without. You'll even learn how to save money while shopping for keto ingredients, freeze fully-made keto meals so you can enjoy heat-and-eat dishes later, and cook once to make several meals.

In *The 5-Ingredient Keto Cookbook*, you'll find recipes to enjoy from morning to night, from large meals to small bites. In chapter 3, Staples, Building Blocks, and Big-Batch Recipes, you'll discover create-ahead dishes as well as component pieces that can be used as the foundation of multiple healthy meals .You'll also learn how to use your slow

cooker and freezer to help with meal prep. In addition, this chapter offers basic recipes (such as for bone broth) that you can build upon and use over and over again.

Chapter 4, Early-Day Keto Meals, covers one of our favorite meals of the day: breakfast. If you've heard that keto breakfasts are all about eggs, you're not wrong. Eggs are one of the most ketogenic-perfect foods around, and people on high-fat diets eat a lot of them. However, you'll find plenty of non-eggy breakfast foods in this chapter to help support your keto eating plan.

Chapter 5, Keto Sips and Slurps, gives you a range of cold and hot drinks—all keto-compliant, all with macro counts—that can be enjoyed from breakfast to after dinner. There are even recipes for all-important electrolyte drinks, which are popular in the keto world to help you reach and maintain ketosis.

In chapter 6, Small Plates and Quick Bites: Lunches and Other Small Meals, you'll find everything from brown-bag gourmet sandwiches to elegant luncheon dishes. I've also included some versatile "blueprints" that help you fashion something yummy to eat based on what is in your kitchen at any given time.

Chapter 7, Fat Bombs and Fatty Snacks, offers recipes for that most important of keto foods: the fat bomb. These delicious, high-fat, low-carb treats ensure that you are consuming enough fat to make it to ketosis. Take a look: You'll find an intriguing lineup of both savory and sweet fat bombs.

Chapter 8, Dinner and Other Large Meals, is chock full of dinner recipes that range from casual to more formal nighttime dishes, featuring meat, fish, and even a few vegetarian options, from light meals to heartier fare.

If you have ever wondered about a certain element of the ketogenic diet, chances are you'll find the answers to your questions about keto cooking, keto eating, and the ins and outs of the keto diet in chapter 9, FAQs.

Don't forget to check out Resources, at the back of the book (including conversion charts!), if you'd like to go deeper and learn more about keto. You'll find a list of books, websites, blogs, podcasts, and even shops, all of which can make your keto eating adventure easier and more fun. There are even conversion charts to make measuring, counting, cooking, and eating on the keto plan easy.

Thank you so much for choosing *The 5-Ingredient Keto Cookbook* to accompany you on your high-fat, low-carb journey! Turn the page, and let's get cooking!

A selection of keto-friendly food makes
a fast, easy, healthy keto meal.

1

KETO EATING

AND

HOW TO USE THIS COOKBOOK

EVEN IF YOU'RE NOT CURRENTLY "EATING KETO," YOU KNOW HOW popular the ketogenic diet is. In 2018, "keto diet" was Google's most-searched diet term, and the international market research firm Technavio predicts that the global keto diet market will grow by USD $1.11 billion by 2023.

N OTHER WORDS, MILLIONS OF people worldwide have either studied the ketogenic eating plan or are eating keto. If you are one of these people, you may already know a thing or two about the ketogenic diet.

Originally developed in the 1920s to help reduce seizures in epileptic patients, the ketogenic plan requires that you count macronutrients (aka "macros"), unlike other diets that involve counting calories, fat grams, and perhaps sugar grams. Macros are the energy-producing components of the diet that include carbohydrates, protein, and fat. In other words, macronutrients are fuel, the nutrients your body needs—in large amounts—to produce the energy you need to live. If you were a car, macronutrients would be the gasoline that helps your motor run. For some who follow the keto diet, consuming too many carb-based macros can lead to weight gain, which is one of the reasons why ketogenic eaters carefully monitor their macros.

IMPORTANT NUMBERS

Percentages You Need to Know

As you may already know, ketogenic diets are high in fat, moderate in protein, and low in carbohydrates. The macronutrient ratio falls within the following ranges:

Generally speaking, 60–75 percent (typically 119–134 grams) of the daily keto diet is made up of fat, 15–30 percent (typically 75–89 grams) comes from protein, and 5–10 percent (typically 20–27 grams) is derived from net carbs.

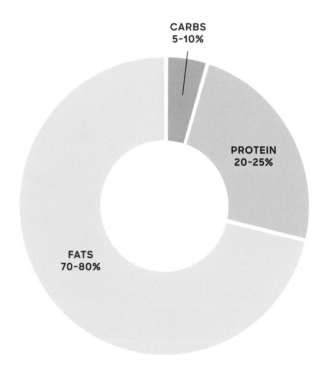

CARBS
5-10%

PROTEIN
20-25%

FATS
70-80%

A quick word about carbs

When you read the nutrition panel on packaged food, chances are you've seen an amount for "Total Carbohydrates" or, simply, "Carbohydrates." In the world of keto, total carbohydrates are not the carbs you count. The only carbs that matter to a keto eater are net carbs. Measured in grams, net carbs are the total carbohydrates consumed, minus all carbs derived from fiber. (While the body does not digest fiber, fiber is vital for cholesterol control and a healthy digestive tract.)

All nutrition labels list a food's total carb count. Unfortunately, however, most do not include a listing for net carbs. Luckily, there's an easy way to calculate a food's net carb count: Subtract the fiber grams from the total carb grams. For example, if a food has 20 grams of total carbs and 15 grams of fiber, your net carb total is 5 grams.

Given keto's popularity, it is no surprise that there are hundreds of resources to help keep you and your macros on track, from keto-newbie blogs, to gargantuan keto bibles that take a deep dive into every nook and cranny of the keto lifestyle, to science-based websites that give you the physiological ins and outs of ketosis. This book does not focus on any of those elements; instead, *The 5-Ingredient Keto Cookbook* supplies

hands-on, practical kitchen assistance and is a resource focused on helping you to quickly, easily, and efficiently make delicious, keto-compliant meals.

In short, *The 5-Ingredient Keto Cookbook* makes keto eating and cooking easy by keeping down the number of ingredients in each recipe while supplying great flavor. Keto cooking can be fussy and time consuming, and, on top of finding (yummy) recipes that contain the right keto-compliant ingredients, there are macros to worry about. Most of us have jam-packed

Nutrition Facts

Serving Size 3 oz. (85g)
Serving Per Container 2

Amount Per Serving

Calories	200	Calories from Fat 120

	% Daily Value*
Total Fat 15g	20 %
Saturated Fat 5g	28 %
Trans Fat 3g	
Cholesterol 30mg	10 %
Sodium 650mg	28 %
Total Carbohydrate 30g	10 %
Dietary Fiber 0g	0 %
Sugars 5g	
Protein 5g	

Vitamin A 5%	●	Vitamin C 2%
Calcium 15%	●	Iron 5%

*Percent Daily Values are based on a 2,000 calorie diet. Your Daily Values may be higher or lower depending on your calorie needs.

	Calories	2,000	2,500
Total Fat	Less than	65g	80g
Sat Fat	Less than	20g	25g
Cholesterol	Less than	300mg	300mg
Sodium	Less than	2,400mg	2,400mg
Total Carbohydrate		300mg	375mg
Dietary Fiber		25g	30g

Keep keto-friendly ingredients like these on hand for easy keto cooking.

schedules. Who wants to spend precious hours with their calculator, trying to figure out how many net grams of carbs, or fat, or protein, a recipe has? *The 5-Ingredient Keto Cookbook* has done that for you. Each recipe is keto compliant and (for your convenience!) lists macros, so you can plug the numbers into your daily menus.

In the pages of this book, you'll find recipes. More than 100 recipes—everything from keto drinks and fat bombs to breakfasts and slow-cooker dinners (and everything in between). Every recipe contains five ingredients (or, in some cases, fewer) and can easily be prepared, even by novice cooks. You'll also find advice on how to set up your keto kitchen, cook in bulk, freeze and pack keto meals, and so much more.

About those five ingredients . . .

The recipes in *The 5-Ingredient Keto Cookbook* do, in fact, contain five (and sometimes fewer) ingredients. However, you will come across some recipes that contain additional ingredients that are optional—extras like garnishes, flavorings, and seasonings (salt, pepper, spices, and herbs). What all this means for you, dear keto cook, is that you have the option to add these lovely extra ingredients at your own discretion.

An important note about the keto diet

As you know, the keto diet encourages fat consumption and discourages the consumption of carbs. In addition, it requires that you count macros and measure ketones daily. As a result of these often-complicated tasks, a dedicated culture—complete with keto food and supplement companies, educational websites, blogs, apps, magazines, trade shows, and even clubs—has cropped up to help keto eaters establish and maintain ketosis, the basis of the diet.

The 5-Ingredient Keto Cookbook is a cookbook, not a scientific work focused on the science of keto. But because your overall health is important, I advise you to speak with your doctor before beginning the keto diet. If you are pregnant or have an underlying health condition, the keto diet may not be for you. With so much information online, including hundreds of keto-related blogs, it is tempting to skip this step. In the strongest terms, I urge you not to start the keto diet until you've met with a doctor.

2

SETTING UP YOUR PANTRY

BEING STRATEGIC ABOUT THE FOOD AND EQUIPMENT YOU HAVE IN your kitchen can make meal prep, brown bag lunch packing, cooking, snacking—and anything else having to do with food—so much easier, faster, and less exhausting. In this chapter, you'll find out about what you need to make keto cooking as easy and fast as possible!

KETO Food Staples

Stocking your kitchen with a variety of keto-compliant ingredients (and a few keto convenience foods for those times when you just can't make food from scratch) is essential to your ketogenic success. Fortunately, keto staples are familiar foods that you may already have in your fridge, freezer, and pantry. Take a look at this list—and remember, feel free to pass on anything for which you have an intolerance or allergy or that you just don't enjoy eating:

Red Meat
* Beef, ground (preferably 80 percent or 85 percent lean)
* Flank steak
* Roast chuck
* Sirloin
* Pork butt
* Pork chop
* Pork loin
* Pork shoulder
* Prosciutto
* Uncured bacon
* Sausage (Italian, Mexican chorizo, breakfast, kielbasa, etc.)
* Dried, cured sausage (Spanish chorizo, pepperoni, salami, etc.)
* Liverwurst
* Lamb chop
* Lamb roast
* Lamb shank

Poultry
* Chicken breast
* Chicken thigh
* Chicken drumstick
* Chicken, whole
* Turkey breast
* Turkey drumstick
* Turkey, whole
* Other poultry (duck, goose, grouse, pheasant, quail, etc.)
* Eggs

Fish and Seafood
* Bluefish
* Calamari/squid (unbreaded)
* Octopus
* Salmon (steaks and fillets)
* Shellfish (clams, mussels, oysters)
* Shrimp, and other crustaceans, including crab, lobster, crawfish, etc
* Smoked fish (salmon, whitefish, trout, etc.)
* Tuna (steaks and fillets)
* White fish (haddock, cod, skate, etc.)

Dairy
* Butter (unsalted or salted)
* Cheese (hard and soft varieties)
* Cream cheese, Neufchatel, Marscapone
* Ghee (liquid butter from which the milk solids have been removed)
* Heavy cream (also known as whipping cream)
* Yogurt (full fat/whole milk, unflavored, traditional, or Greek)

Vegetables (fresh or frozen)

* Asparagus
* Avocado
* Cabbage (Brussels sprouts, bok choy, napa, etc.)
* Cauliflower
* Celery
* Chile pepper (jalapeño, poblano, serrano, etc.)
* Cucumber
* Eggplant
* Lettuce (any variety)
* Spinach (baby, regular)
* Spaghetti squash
* Summer squash (crookneck, yellow, and zucchini)

Fruit (fresh or frozen; used *very* sparingly)

* Blackberries
* Cranberries
* Raspberries
* Fresh lemons
* Fresh limes

Snacks

* Oil-cured olives (Kalamata, Niçoise, etc.)
* Jerky (beef, venison, elk, bison, salmon, turkey, etc.)
* Pork rinds
* Cheese chips, frico, etc.

Pantry Staples

* Almond flour
* Coconut flour
* Canned, aseptic boxes, or frozen bone broth/stock (chicken, beef, fish)
* Coconut milk (*avoid lite or light coconut milk*)
* Coconut cream
* Extra-virgin olive oil
* Coconut oil
* Avocado oil
* Tuna packed in oil
* Salmon packed in oil
* Sardines
* Anchovies
* Herring
* Stevia (granulated or liquid)
* Coconut (unsweetened flaked)
* Coconut butter
* Cacao butter

Seasonings

* Garlic powder
* Onion powder
* Spices of your choice
* Dried herbs of your choice
* Pink Himalayan salt
* Pepper/peppercorns (black, pink, green, red, etc.)

Condiments

* Hot sauce (Tabasco)
* Prepared mustard (brown, whole-grain, yellow) (*Note*: Avoid "flavored" mustards, which have carbs and sugars, such as honey, chipotle, wasabi, horseradish, sriracha, etc.)
* Mayonnaise (avoid reduced-fat or light)
* Dill pickles
* Capers (in brine, oil, or salt)

Convenience Items

* Cauliflower rice
* Broccoli rice
* Cauliflower pizza crust
* Mashed cauliflower
* Spiralized zucchini

Freezing Foods

A freezer packed with keto-compliant food means you can make a meal quickly. One of the easiest and most economical ways of stocking your freezer with low-carb meals is to freeze uneaten portions of keto meals in individual-size serving containers (these leftovers make fantastic, fast grab-and-go lunches). If you're unsure about how to freeze foods, here are a few tips:

* All meat, poultry, fish, and some dairy (such as cheese) can be frozen. Though there are many ways to prepare food for freezing, I prefer the "double wrap" method: First, wrap individual portions of food in waxed paper or plastic freezer wrap, and then wrap the outer layer in heavy foil. Alternatively, you can place the item in a freezerproof container and then wrap it in a layer of foil, just to make sure everything remains airtight and fresh. Then, place a piece of tape on the wrapped item and, with a permanent marker, make a note of what is in the package, the date it was frozen, and the "use by" date (about three months out).

* All cooked meals in *The 5-Ingredient Keto Cookbook* can be placed in freezerproof containers and frozen. (I would not recommend freezing bowls or salads, but anything else that is not meant to be eaten immediately can be frozen.)

* There are many types of food that you might not realize can be frozen, including: shredded cheese, blocks of cheese, ripe Hass avocado (one method is to store mashed avocados in small containers), individual raw eggs that have been cracked into freezerproof containers, and small amounts of canned sauces, condiments, coconut milk, whole milk, half-and-half, or whipping cream.

* To thaw previously frozen food, place it in the refrigerator. Most items will thaw in 8 to 24 hours.

Keto Equipment

Eating the ketogenic way can be so much easier if you have these kitchen helpers:

CALCULATOR If you are terrible at math, as I am, a handy calculator nearby will help you tally up macros easily.

DIGITAL SCALE When you're eyeballing ingredients, it's easy to guess wrong. Normally, this isn't a big deal, but when you're trying to attain ketosis, being an ounce or two off with your ingredients can keep you from reaching or maintaining your goal.

SILICONE BAKEWARE Due to the lack of structure-giving ingredients, keto recipes can sometimes be a bit fragile. Silicone baking mats, muffin cups, and other bakeware ensures that what you make doesn't end up in crumbs.

SPIRALIZER (OR A SPIRALIZER ATTACHMENT FOR YOUR STAND MIXER OR FOOD PROCESSOR) Although you can probably purchase spiralized zucchini at your local market, it's expensive and not always fresh. This kitchen essential makes veggie noodles quickly—and it's fun to use, too!

SLOW COOKER Big cuts of meat are transformed into delicious pulled pork, chicken, and brisket for sandwiches or keto bowls with this must-have appliance. Plus, you'll want to start making your own bone broth with all those bones, right? Toss them in the slow cooker, cover them with water and a generous sprinkling of salt, set the timer for 10 hours, and go about your life.

ALUMINUM FOIL Lots of aluminum foil. It makes cleanup a breeze when you line pans with foil.

LIQUID MEASURING CUP Precision is important in keto cooking. A liquid measuring cup allows you to measure fluid ounces, milliliters, and cups.

MEASURING CUPS, AKA "DRY MEASURES" AND MEASURING SPOONS I'll bet you already have these.

A zucchini quickly transforms into low-carb noodles when spiralized.

50 Foods That Are Best to Avoid

While I dislike the idea of forbidding any food, even I must admit that there are many foods that just aren't worth the macros. Here is my own "don't bring these into your kitchen" list.

NOTE There are many books, charts, apps and websites where you can find a food's macros, each of which will give you slightly different results. The results below were found using The Food Calorie Calculator (at https://caloriecontrol.org/healthy-weight-tool-kit/food-calorie-calculator/), powered by the USDA Nutrient Database, and, where necessary, the Food Calorie Counter & Calculator (https://www.webmd.com/diet/healthtool-food-calorie-counter) , from Webmd.com:

True Grains and Grainlike Seeds

1. **Amaranth** Average net carb count per ½ cup serving of cooked amaranth: 55 g

2. **Barley** Average net carb count per ½ cup serving of cooked barley: 19.6 g

3. **Buckwheat** Average net carb count per ½ cup serving of cooked buckwheat groats: 14.5 g

4. **Corn (including popcorn, tortilla chips, corn on the cob, polenta, etc.)** Average net carb count per 1 ear serving of corn on the cob: 14.7 g

5. **Millet** Average net carb count per ½ cup serving of cooked millet: 19.3 g

6. **Oats (including oatmeal, granola, etc.)** Average net carb count per ½ cup serving of cooked oatmeal: 11 g

7. **Quinoa** Average net carb count per ½ cup serving of cooked quinoa: 20 g

8. **Rice (white, brown, wild, arborio, etc.)** Average net carb count per serving of ½ cup serving of white rice: 22 g

9. **Teff (including injera, etc.)** Average net carb count per ½ cup serving of cooked teff: 25 g

10. **Wheat (and wheat-related grains and foods, including spelt, rye, semolina, farina, couscous, pasta, bread, etc.)** Average net carb count per 1 piece serving of whole-wheat bread: 10 g

Beans and Legumes

11. **Beans (kidney, cannellini, navy, pink, black beans, black-eyed peas, etc.)** Average net carb count per 1-cup serving of cooked pinto beans: 25.5 g

12. **Broad beans (butter, broad, limas, etc.)** Average net carb count per 1-cup serving of cooked lima beans: 26 g

13. **Garbanzo beans (chickpeas)** Average net carb count per 1-cup serving of cooked garbanzo beans: 35 g

14. **Lentils (brown, red, black, French, etc.)** Average net carb count per 1-cup serving of cooked brown lentils: 22.2 g

15. **Mung beans** Average net carb count per 1-cup serving of cooked mung beans: 28.4 g

16. **Peas (split green, yellow)** Average net carb count per 1-cup serving of cooked green split peas: 25 g

Fruit

Due to their high carb counts, it is best to avoid all fruit, other than the ones listed on the Keto STAPLES list

Here's a list of the worst offenders:

17. **Apple** Average net carb count per one medium apple: 16.3 g

18. **Banana** Average net carb count per one medium banana: 23.5 g

19. **Cantaloupe** Average net carb count per 1-cup serving: 12 g

20. **Cherry** Average net carb count per 1-cup serving: 16.5 g

21. **Fig** Average net carb count per one medium fig: 8 g

22. **Grape** Average net carb count per 1-cup serving: 28 g

23. **Honeydew melon** Average net carb count per 1-cup serving: 14 g

24. **Kiwi** Average net carb count per one medium kiwi: 9.8 g

25. **Mango** Average net carb count per one medium mango: 25 g

26. **Papaya** Average net carb count per 1-cup serving: 11.5 g

27. **Pear** Average net carb count per one medium pear: 20.5 g

28. **Peach** Average net carb count per one medium peach: 12.5 g

29. **Pineapple** Average net carb count per 1-cup serving: 18 g

30. **Plum** Average net carb count per one medium plum: 8.5 g

Fruit Juice

It is best to avoid all fruit juice. Here's a list of popular offenders.

31. **Apple juice** Average net carb count per 8 ounce serving: 28 g

32. **Cranberry juice cocktail** Average net carb per 8 ounce serving: 28 g

33. **Grape juice** Average net carb count per 8 ounce serving: 37.2 g

34. **Orange juice** Average net carb count per 8 ounce serving: 27.4 g

35. **Pineapple juice** Average net carb per 8 ounce serving: 32.13 g

Vegetables

With so many low-carb veggies to choose from, there is no reason to overdo the high-carb varieties. Here are a few that I suggest enjoying in moderation or avoiding outright.

36. **Beet** Average net carb count per 1 cup serving: 10 g

37. **Carrot** Average net carb count per 1-cup serving: 9 g

38. **Corn** Aerage net carb count per 1-cup serving: 36 g

39. **Green pea** Average net carb count per 1 cup serving: 28 g

40. **Jerusalem artichoke** Average net carb count per 1 cup serving: 24.12 g

41. **Parsnip** Average net carb count per 1-cup serving: 21 g

42. **Pumpkin/Winter squash** Average net carb count per 1-cup serving: 14 g

43. **Sweet poato** Average net carb count per 1-cup serving of baked sweet potato: 35 g

44. **White potato (russet, Idaho, red, Yukon Gold, etc.)** Average net carb count per one medium potato: 33.9 g

Dried Fruit

It is best to avoid all dried fruit. Here's a list of the worst offenders.

45. **Date** Average net carb count per five-date serving: 27 g

46. **Dried apricots** Average net carb count per five-dried-apricot serving: 19 g

47. **Dried cranberries (sweetened)** Average net carb count per ⅓ cup serving: 31 g

48. **Dried fig** Average net carb count per five-dried-fig serving: 27 g

49. **Prune** Average net carb count per five-prune serving: 21 g

50. **Raisin** Average net carb count per ¼ cup serving: 31 g

3

STAPLES, BUILDING BLOCKS, AND BIG-BATCH RECIPES

IF YOU'RE LOOKING FOR SOME ADVICE THAT WILL MAKE KETO

cooking and eating easier than you ever thought possible, here

it is, in two words: batch cook. Cooking large amounts of food

in batches allows you to dole it out into individual portions and

use those portions as stand-alone meals or as building blocks

to make other delicious, fast keto dishes. This chapter features

many basic recipes for keto staples that you can quickly fash-

ion into yummy keto meals later in the week or (if you freeze

portions) later in the month. Because the easier keto cooking is

for you, the more likely you're going to keep eating keto. Makes

sense, right?

Make-Ahead Bacon

Makes about 4 servings

1 pound uncooked thin- or thick-sliced bacon, (I prefer nitrite-free uncured bacon)

A few years ago, when precooked bacon began showing up in grocery stores, I couldn't help but make fun of it. (If memory serves, premade frozen peanut butter and jelly sandwiches appeared around the same time—I made fun of those, too!) But if I am being honest, there are times when I wish bacon would cook faster! So I created my own do-it-yourself way to create precooked bacon. Double or triple (or quadruple) this recipe, if you'd like. Just make sure no bacon slices overlap while you're cooking!)

1. Preheat the oven to 400°F. (If you have a convection oven, I encourage you to use it; set it to 375°F.)

2. Arrange as much bacon as you can, slices not touching and in a single layer, on one, two, or three rimmed baking sheets. (They must be rimmed, or the bacon grease can run into the oven). Some people like to line their baking sheets with foil first, but I've never felt the need.

3. Bake the bacon for 15 to 25 minutes, depending on how soft or crispy you like it.

4. Remove the baking sheet(s) from the oven and allow the bacon to rest on the baking sheet(s) for 5 minutes before removing it with tongs and arranging it on a serving plate. The bacon will keep in the refrigerator (up to a week) or freezer (up to 3 months) in a covered container.

Macros per 4 thin slices of cooked bacon: 108 calories, 0.3 g net carbs, 0.3 g total carbs, 0 g fiber, 0 g sugars, 8.4 g total fat, 7.4 g protein

Keto Bouncy Eggs

Makes 6 servings

6 tablespoons water

6 large eggs

This is a great easy recipe for poached eggs—a lot of them. You'll need a standard six-cup muffin pan here, but you can also double the recipe and use a twelve-cup muffin pan without altering the time or temperature. Enjoy!

1. Preheat the oven to 350°F.

2. Add 1 tablespoon of water to each cup in a 6-cup muffin tin.

3. Crack 1 large egg into each cup and gently place the pan in the oven.

4. Cook for 11 to 13 minutes, depending on how runny or set you like your eggs. Gently remove the muffin tin from the oven and spoon out the eggs, one at a time.

5. You may notice a minute bit of water on top of the eggs. It is easy to mistake this for uncooked egg white, but it truly is water. Ignore it and gently lift the eggs out of the muffin cups using a soup spoon. Any water will drip off as you lift out the eggs.

6. Enjoy the eggs immediately or allow them to cool and then place them in an air-tight container and store in the refrigerator for up to three days.

Macros per serving: 77.5 calories, 0.4 g net carbs, 0.4 g total carbs, 0 g fiber, 0.6 g sugars, 4.8 g total fat, 6.3 g protein

Make-Ahead Quiche Bites

Makes 12 servings

Oil for greasing muffin cups

1½ cups shredded sharp cheddar cheese

10 strips Make-Ahead Bacon (see page 16), crumbled or minced

12 large eggs

¼ cup half-and-half or heavy cream

OPTIONAL

Salt and pepper, to taste

½ to 1 tablespoon minced fresh herbs

This easy recipe for a dozen "eggy bites" makes the perfect grab-and-go keto snack. Feel free to use a different type of cheese, add some of your favorite herbs or spices, and change up (or omit) the meat. You can even toss in up to a half cup of minced cooked veggies. You'll need a twelve-cup muffin tin for this recipe.

1. Preheat oven to 400°F.

2. Generously coat a muffin pan with softened butter or an oil of your choice.

3. Divide the cheese and bacon evenly between the empty muffin cups.

4. In a medium bowl, whisk together the eggs, half-and-half or cream, salt and pepper (if using), and herbs (if using). Divide the egg mixture among the muffin cups, filling them half to three-quarters of the way full.

5. Bake until the muffins are set and lightly browned around the edges, 12 to 14 minutes.

6. Remove the pan from the oven and allow it to cool for 5 minutes.

7. Serve the quiche warm, or allow it to cool and then store it in a covered container in the fridge for up to 3 days.

8. For longer storage, place the quiche bites in an airtight container or freezer storage bag and freeze for up to 3 months.

Macros per serving (made with half-and-half and optional ingredients): 216 calories, 0.9 g net carbs, 0.9 g total carbs, 0 g fiber, 0 g sugars, 16.4 g total fat, 15.7 g protein

Perfect Hard-Boiled Eggs

Makes 8 servings

8 eggs

Do you need a recipe for hard-boiled eggs? Maybe not, but this method lets you make as many perfect hard-boiled eggs as you'd like, whether it's one egg or a dozen. This recipe works best with medium, large, and extra-large eggs.

1. Place the eggs in a 2-quart saucepan that is wide enough to keep the eggs from touching one another. Cover the eggs with 1 inch of cool water.

2. Slowly bring the water to a boil over medium heat; when the water has reached a boil, cover the pot and remove it from the heat.

3. For extra-large eggs, let the saucepan sit for 14 to 16 minutes, depending on how hard you like the yolk. Let large eggs sit 10 to 12 minutes. For medium eggs, the sitting time is 6 to 8 minutes.

4. Transfer the eggs to a colander in the sink and let cold water run over them to stop the cooking process. You can even plunge the eggs into an ice bath, which some people say makes them easier to peel later. Serve the eggs immediately or place them in a container or egg carton in the fridge for up to a week.

Macros per 1 large egg: 77.5 calories, 0.4 g net carbs, 0.4 g total carbs, 0 g fiber, 0.6 g sugars, 4.8 g total fat, 6.3 g protein

Keto Sheet Eggs

Makes 4 or 5 servings

Unsalted butter or oil,
to grease the pan

9 large eggs

3 tablespoons cream, half-
and-half, or whole milk

Salt and pepper, to taste

This is an unusual—and awesome—egg recipe. You use a blender to whip up the eggs, then pour them onto a rimmed baking sheet. The finished product almost looks like a thin sheet cake that you can cut into squares for sandwiches, nestle into greens, or stack with other ingredients.

1. Preheat the oven to 350°F.

2. Grease a 13 x 9-inch rimmed (it must be rimmed!) baking sheet. Set it aside.

3. Place all the ingredients in a blender and process until everything is well combined.

4. Place the prepared baking sheet on an oven rack in the middle of the oven and carefully pour in the egg mixture. (If you pour the eggs into the pan first, there's a good chance it will splash out of the pan while you're transferring it to the oven.)

5. Bake the eggs until they're just set in the middle, about 8 minutes.

6. Allow the eggs to cool and set in the pan for 10 minutes before cutting them into 4 or 5 portions.

7. You can store the eggs in a single layer in an airtight container in the refrigerator for up to 3 days.

Macros per serving: 176 calories, 1 g net carbs, 1 g total carbs, 0 g fiber, 0.9 g sugars, 12.9 g total fat, 14.2 g protein

Sunny-Side-Up Sheet Eggs

Makes 12 servings

Butter or oil, to grease
the pan

12 eggs

Salt and pepper, to taste

This is another "why didn't I think of that before?" recipe that is brilliant in its simplicity and efficiency. You are going to love this way of making "sunny side up eggs" in volume! (If you want to make just a few eggs, use a smaller pan.)

1. Preheat the oven to 425°F.

2. Grease a rimmed (it must be rimmed!) 13 x 9-inch baking sheet and place it in the oven (without the eggs) for 10 to 20 minutes 'til it's hot (don't skip this step!).

3. While the baking sheet is heating up, gently crack the eggs into a lipped bowl or pitcher (a large liquid measuring cup works beautifully). As you crack the eggs, be careful not to break any of the egg yolks. Set the bowl aside.

4. Remove the baking sheet from the oven and gently pour the eggs onto the pan.

5. Sprinkle the eggs with salt and pepper and gingerly slide the pan back into the oven.

6. Bake the eggs for about 4 or 5 minutes, or until the whites are beginning to set but the yolks are still runny.

7. Gently remove the pan from the oven and place it on the counter; the eggs will firm up a bit once they're out of the oven.

8. To serve, use a thin, metal spatula and score the eggs into 12 individual servings. Gently transfer the eggs to serving plates. The eggs don't hold up well, so eat them immediately.

Macros per serving: 84 calories, 0.4 g net carbs, 0.4 g total carbs, 0 g fiber, 0.4 g sugars, 6.4 g total fat, 6.3 g protein

Chicken Bone Broth

Makes about 3 quarts

1 (4-pound) chicken, whole; or the carcasses of 2 or 3 chickens (parts or whole, such as from a rotisserie chicken)

1 medium onion, quartered

2 stalks celery, quartered

1 to 2 tablespoons salt (start with 1 tablespoon and adjust with more at the end of cooking)

OPTIONAL

1 teaspoon whole black peppercorns

1 to 3 scallions and/or 1 leek, white and/or green parts (the green parts of scallions and leeks are great used in the stockpot. Just be absolutely sure the scallions and leeks are cleaned of any grit before adding to the stockpot)

Parsley stems, whole thyme sprigs, fennel fronds, bay leaf

This is a great beginner's recipe for bone broth that can be enjoyed on its own or used as an ingredient to create a lovely chicken broth. To add even greater depth of flavor to the broth, use leftover bones from chicken parts and whole chickens that you've frozen and stored in airtight containers, ready for use whenever you need them.

1. Place all the ingredients in a large stockpot and cover with about 4 quarts of water, or until all ingredients are covered by about 1 inch of water.

2. Place the pot over high heat, cover with a lid, and cook until the liquid comes to a rolling boil.

3. Reduce the heat to a low simmer and cook for 4 hours. If desired, skim off any fat that collects on the top during the cooking process.

4. After 4 hours, turn off the heat and allow the broth to cool in the pot for 90 minutes or more.

5. Carefully remove all the solids, using a skimmer or spider strainer, or pour the broth into a colander set over a large bowl.

6. Decant the broth into 1 cup containers for individual servings.

7. Store the broth in the fridge for up to 3 days. If you want to keep it longer, place it in an airtight container in the freezer for up to 3 months.

Macros per 1 cup serving (made with optional ingredients): 17 calories, 0.9 g net carbs, 0.9 g total carbs, 0 g fiber, 0 g sugars, 1 g total fat, 3.3 g protein

Beef Bone Broth

Makes 3 quarts

4 pounds beef shank or neck bones (or whatever you have on hand)

1 medium onion, quartered

2 stalks celery, quartered

1 to 2 tablespoons salt (start with 1 tablespoon and adjust with more at the end of cooking)

OPTIONAL

1 teaspoon whole black peppercorns

1 to 3 scallions and/or 1 leek, green parts only (be absolutely sure the scallions and leeks are cleaned of any grit before adding to the stockpot)

Parsley stems, whole thyme sprigs, fennel fronds, bay leaf

For you beef lovers, here's a broth recipe made from beef bones. Feel free to swap in a few pork bones, if you have them.

1. Place all the ingredients in a large stockpot and cover with about 4 quarts of water, or until all ingredients are covered by about 1 inch of water.

2. Place the pot over high heat, cover with a lid, and cook until the liquid comes to a rolling boil.

3. Reduce the heat to a low simmer and cook for 4 hours. If desired, skim off any fat that collects on the top during the cooking process.

4. After 4 hours, turn off the heat and allow broth to cool in the pot for 90 minutes or more.

5. Carefully remove all the solids, using a skimmer or spider strainer, or pour the broth into a colander set over a large bowl.

6. Decant the broth into 1 cup containers for individual servings.

7. Store the broth in the fridge for up to 3 days. If you want to keep it longer, place in an airtight container in the freezer for up to 3 months.

Macros per 1 cup serving (made with optional ingredients): 70 calories, 1 g net carbs, 1 g total carbs, 0 g fiber, 0 g sugars, 4 g total fat, 6 g protein

Keto Vinaigrette

Makes about 1 pint

1⅓ cups extra-virgin olive oil, avocado oil, or other oil

1 cup balsamic vinegar, sherry, red wine, or other vinegar

1 teaspoon salt, or to taste

OPTIONAL

1 to 2 teaspoons Dijon mustard, or another type of mustard

¼ to ½ teaspoon garlic powder or onion powder

¼ to ½ teaspoon dried or powdered herbs or spices, such as basil, thyme, or oregano

Everyone needs a good, basic salad dressing. Enjoy this one as is or use the optional ingredients for additional flavor. You can also swap in a different type of vinegar or oil, if you like.

1. Combine everything in a pint (or larger) jar.

2. Screw on the lid and shake well.

3. Store the vinaigrette in the fridge for up to 2 months. Shake before using.

Macros per 1 tablespoon serving (made with extra-virgin olive oil and balsamic vinegar and optional ingredients): 75 calories, 0.5 g net carbs, 0.5 g total carbs, 0 g fiber, 0 g sugars, 8 g total fat, 0 g protein

Low-Carb Hummus

Makes about 4 cups

4 cups steamed cauliflower florets or peeled and chopped raw zucchini

¾ cup tahini (sesame paste)

½ cup fresh lemon juice

¼ cup extra-virgin olive oil

4 garlic cloves

OPTIONAL

Salt and pepper, to taste

1 tablespoon ground cumin

Like me, you may have relied on hummus and veggies as a healthy snack in your pre-keto days, only to discover that it is forbidden on the keto diet. That's because hummus is very carb heavy. Fortunately, there is a keto workaround: you can swap in steamed cauliflower or raw zucchini for the traditional chickpeas.

1. Combine all the ingredients (including optional ingredients, if you're using them) in a blender and puree until the mixture is thick and smooth.

2. Taste the hummus and adjust the seasonings to your liking.

3. Store for up to 1 week in a covered container in the fridge. (This recipe doesn't freeze well.)

Macros per ¼-cup serving (made with optional ingredients): 130 calories, 2.5 g net carbs, 2.5 g total carbs, 0 g fiber, 0 g sugars, 14 g total fat, 2 g protein

Stay-Fresh Keto Guacamole

Makes about 2 cups

2 large, ripe Hass avocados, peeled and pitted

½ small jalapeño, stem and seeds removed, minced (add more or less, to taste)

1 tablespoon fresh lime juice

¼ teaspoon salt

OPTIONAL

¼ cup finely chopped fresh cilantro

Pinch of cumin

Pinch of garlic powder

Dash of hot sauce

Thank goodness avocado is a keto favorite! Hello, guacamole! This make-ahead version features a healthy dose of lime juice, which helps keep it fresh for 2 days in the fridge.

1. Place all the ingredients in a bowl and mash with a fork until the mixture is smooth and well combined.

2. Tightly cover the bowl with plastic wrap, making sure the plastic touches and covers the entire surface of the guacamole. This will keep the avocado from oxidizing and turning brown. Refrigerate the guacamole for up to 2 days before serving.

Macros per ½-cup serving (made without optional ingredients): 207 calories, 2.4 g net carbs, 9.2 g total carbs, 6.8 g fiber, 0.7 g sugars, 19.6 g total fat, 2 g protein

Avocado Mayo

Makes about 1½ cups

½ cup mayonnaise

1 Hass avocado, peeled and pitted

OPTIONAL

¼ cup chopped fresh cilantro, dill, parsley, chives, or a combination

2 teaspoons lime juice

Salt and pepper, to taste

Rich in eggs and oil, mayonnaise is the perfect keto ingredient. Combine it with avocado, another perfect keto ingredient, and you've got yourself the most divine low-carb, high-fat condiment ever! If you don't have lime juice, lemon juice works just as well.

1. Add the mayonnaise, avocado, cilantro, and lime juice to a food processor or blender and process until smooth.

2. Add salt and pepper, to taste.

Macros per 2-tablespoon serving (made with optional ingredients): 73 calories, 2.8 g net carbs, 3.9 g total carbs, 1.1 g fiber, 0.7 g sugars, 6.5 g total fat, 0.4 g protein

Sandwich Salad
BLUEPRINT

Makes about 1½ cups (3 generous servings)

2 tablespoons mayonnaise

1 to 3 teaspoons prepared mustard (Dijon, brown, grainy; please avoid honey mustard or any other sweetened mustard)

Salt and pepper, to taste

1½ cups chopped or flaked protein of your choice (such as poultry, canned fish or seafood, red meat, or Perfect Hard-Boiled Eggs [see page 20])

OPTIONAL

1 to 2 tablespoons chopped fresh herbs (minced dill, parsley, cilantro, chives, etc.)

Pinch of cayenne, curry powder, chile powder, or another spice

Sandwich salad is not really "salad"—at least not in the sense of a green salad. It consists of a protein-rich sandwich filling (that can also be mounded on a plate of greens). Whether you prefer chicken salad, egg salad, white-fish salad, or any other, this easy blueprint lets you make a tasty, nutritious, keto-approved sandwich salad no matter what kind of protein you have on hand.

1. In a large bowl, whisk together the mayonnaise, mustard, salt and pepper, and herbs and spices (if using).

2. Gently fold in the protein, until all ingredients are combined.

3. Serve with a keto-approved wrap (see page 82) or bun (see page 89) or on top of salad greens. Store any remaining sandwich salad in a container in the fridge for up to 3 days.

Macros per ½-cup serving: Calorie, fat, protein, and carb counts will vary with what you decide to use in your sandwich salad.

Keto Cheese Wrappers

Makes 1 wrap

2 slices deli-style cheese, any variety (cheddar, provolone, American, etc.)

NOTE If you'd like to make several cheese wraps ahead, you can stack them between sheets of parchment or waxed paper and store them in a covered container in the fridge for up to three days.

This super-fast, super-easy, super-cheesy recipe requires just one ingredient: cheese slices. It's a fun way to make a quick keto wrapper, which you can then fill with any kind of keto filling you'd like! You'll need parchment paper or waxed paper for this recipe, a rolling pin, and a microwave.

1. Tear off two large pieces of parchment paper. Place one piece on a flat surface and set the other aside.

2. Lay one slice of cheese in the middle of the parchment.

3. Cut the second slice of cheese into four horizontal strips. Lay one strip at the top of the cheese slice, one strip on the left side, one strip on the right side, and one strip at the bottom.

4. Carefully lift the parchment paper with the cheese on it into a microwave and cook on the high setting for 12 to 15 seconds, or until the cheese has begun to get soft and a little bit melty. (Be careful not to overcook!)

5. Lift out the parchment paper with the cheese and place it on the kitchen counter.

6. Lay the reserved piece of parchment paper over the cheese and, using a rolling pin, roll the cheese into one large disk. You can use the palm of your hand, as well, if you find it's easier to shape the soft cheese.

7. Allow the cheese to cool on the kitchen counter and remove both pieces of parchment paper.

Macros per serving (made using cheddar cheese): 160 calories, 0 g net carbs, 0 g total carbs, 0 g fiber, 0 g sugars, 14 g total fat, 10 g protein

Homemade Liver Pâté

Makes 6 servings

20 ounces chicken livers, trimmed of sinew and excess fat, drained

1½ cups whole milk

4 tablespoons unsalted butter

¼ cup heavy cream

Salt and pepper, to taste

OPTIONAL

2 tablespoons brandy

NOTE For an optional clarified-butter topping to keep the pâté fresh, melt 4 ounces of butter in a pan. Slowly bring the butter to a boil and skim off the froth. When no more froth has formed, let the clarified butter cool, then pour it directly over the top of the pâté before refrigerating.

Pâté, liverwurst, Braunschweiger . . . no matter what you call it, this smooth liver spread is a high-end favorite that is keto compliant and easy to make!

1. Place the livers in a large bowl and cover them with the milk. Allow the livers to soak for 30 minutes to 1 hour.

2. Remove the livers and pat them dry with paper towels.

3. Melt the butter in a large skillet over medium-high heat. Fry the livers for no longer than 2 minutes on each side. The center should still be pink. Do not overcook!

4. Place the chicken livers and any butter that is left in the skillet into a food processor, together with the brandy, if you choose to use it, heavy cream, and salt and pepper.

5. Process the mixture until it is smooth. If you want a silky-smooth texture, press the mixture through a fine sieve.

6. Transfer the pâté to a serving dish and place it in the fridge. Cover with plastic wrap, making sure the plastic lays directly on the surface of the pâté. This will help prevent discoloration. Keep the pâté in the fridge for up 10 days.

Macros per serving (made without optional ingredients): 283 calories, 4 g net carbs, 4 g total carbs, 0 g, fiber, 2.8 g sugars, 17.7 g total fat, 25.3 g protein

Make-Ahead Chicken

Makes about 6 servings

⅓ cup melted butter (or avocado oil, bacon fat, coconut oil, extra-virgin olive oil, or macadamia nut oil), (plus extra to grease the pan)

3½ to 4 pounds chicken thighs (bone-in or boneless) or drumsticks or wings (with or without skin)

3 to 8 garlic cloves, minced

2 tablespoons soy sauce

Pinch of salt

OPTIONAL

Black pepper or red pepper flakes, to taste

½ teaspoon dried herbs or 2 teaspoons minced fresh herbs of choice

Making a batch of these chicken thighs (or drumsticks or wings) not only ensures that you are getting something healthy to eat, but it also gives you building blocks for many other recipes in this book. This recipe yields two large or three small thighs per serving.

1. Preheat the oven to 425°F.

2. Lightly grease a large baking pan with a bit of melted butter or your oil or fat of choice.

3. In a medium bowl, whisk together the butter (or oil or bacon fat), garlic, soy sauce, salt, and optional ingredients.

4. Arrange the chicken on the baking pan. Pour the butter mixture over the chicken, coating the pieces thoroughly.

5. Bake the chicken for 25 minutes. Then turn the chicken, basting the pieces with the pan juices.

6. Return the baking dish to the oven and bake for an additional 20 minutes, or until the juices run clear.

7. Remove the pan from the oven and allow the chicken to cool before placing it in a covered container. Keep in the refrigerator for up to 5 days.

Macros per serving (made with bone-in chicken thighs, butter, and optional ingredients): 379 calories, 0.8 g net carbs, 0.9 g total carbs, 0.1 g fiber, 0.1 g sugars, 20.7 g total fat, 52.1 g protein

As-Much-As-You-Want-to-Make Slow Cooker Chicken

Makes about 12 servings

½ cup Chicken Bone Broth (page 24) or water

3 to 4 pounds frozen or fresh boneless chicken breasts or boneless chicken thighs, or a combination of the two (either skinless or skin-on is fine)

¼ to ⅓ cup extra-virgin olive oil or another oil of your choice

1 teaspoon garlic powder (double the amount if you love garlic)

Salt and pepper, to taste

This is one of my favorite recipes in the book because it's just so convenient and—dare I say it?—so cool! All you have to do is put the frozen chicken in the cooker, then return a few hours later, and you have whole pieces of tender chicken to eat as-is, or shred for sandwiches, tacos, or barbecue pulled chicken. Feel free to double or even triple the recipe if you have a large slow cooker.

1. Pour the broth or water into the slow cooker.

2. Place the chicken parts on top of the liquid (there's no need to defrost the chicken if it's frozen).

3. In a small bowl, whisk together the oil, garlic powder, salt, and pepper. Pour the mixture over the chicken in the slow cooker.

4. Turn the slow cooker on low and cook the chicken, if it's frozen, for 4½ to 5 hours (or until the chicken is tender and shreds with a fork); if the chicken is fresh, cook it for 2 hours.

5. Remove the chicken from the cooker and allow it to cool before transferring it to individual-size containers or shredding it in a large bowl with two forks. The chicken will keep in the refrigerator for up to 5 days or up to 3 months in the freezer.

Macros per 1 cup serving (made with chicken breast, water, and ⅓ cup extra-virgin olive oil): 220 calories, 0.1 g net carbs, 0 g total carbs, 0 g fiber, 0 g sugars,
9.3 g total fat, 32 g protein

Slow Cooker Pulled Pork

Makes about 12 servings

1 (3-pound) boneless pork shoulder or butt, sometimes called picnic roast

¼ cup extra-virgin olive oil, avocado oil, or another oil

¼ cup apple cider vinegar

2 teaspoons salt

OPTIONAL

1 teaspoon onion powder

1 teaspoon garlic powder

½ teaspoon black pepper

½ teaspoon paprika

½ teaspoon ground allspice

½ teaspoon celery salt

⅛ teaspoon ground cloves

½ teaspoon mustard powder

If you're intimidated by the idea of making your own pulled pork, I am here to reassure you: It is easy!—especially when you use a slow cooker. Pulled pork freezes well for up to 3 months.

1. Place the pork in a large bowl. Set aside.

2. In a small bowl, whisk together the oil, vinegar, salt, and any optional ingredients.

3. Rub the spice mixture all over the pork. Place the pork roast, fat side up, in the slow cooker and cover.

4. Cook on high for 4 to 6 hours, or until the pork is tender and falling apart.

5. Transfer the roast to a large bowl and shred the meat using two forks. (Add a few tablespoons of the melted fat and liquids to the shredded pork for a moister, fattier, pulled pork.)

6. Serve the shredded pork as is, or with a low-carb barbecue sauce.

7. Store the leftovers in a sealable container in the fridge for up to 1 week.

NOTE There are a lot of optional spices in this recipe. I highly encourage you to not only use them but also add any additional spices or herbs that strike your fancy. An optional, delicious serving suggestion is a drizzle of low-carb barbecue sauce (available at health food stores and keto shopping websites).

Macros per 1 cup serving (made with extra virgin olive oil and optional ingredients): 415 calories, 0.1 g net carbs, 0.1 g total carbs, 0 g fiber, 0 g sugars, 20 g total fat, 38.9 g protein

Keto Slow Cooker Brisket

Makes about 8 servings

1 (4-pound) beef brisket

¼ cup extra-virgin olive oil

Salt and pepper, to taste

2 teaspoons garlic powder

2 cups Beef Bone Broth (see page 25)

OPTIONAL

2 to 4 teaspoons onion powder

1 to 2 teaspoons sweet paprika

Brisket is a versatile dish that can be dressed up for a formal dinner or tucked into a roll for a quick sandwich. This version, which uses a slow cooker, is the epitome of "set it and forget it" cooking!

1. Place the brisket in a large bowl or platter or pan. Set aside.

2. In a small bowl, whisk together the oil, salt and pepper, garlic powder, and optional spices.

3. Rub the oil-spice mixture into the brisket.

4. Pour the broth into the slow cooker.

5. Place the brisket, fatty side facing up, into the broth and cover the slow cooker.

6. Allow the meat to cook for 7 hours on low, or until it is tender. Let the brisket rest in the slow cooker (with the lid off) for an hour or so before serving.

7. For shredded brisket, cut the meat with the grain. For slices of meat, cut the brisket against the grain.

Macros per serving (made with optional ingredients): 380 calories, 0 g net carbs, 0.5 g total carbs, 0 g fiber, 0 g sugars, 20 g total fat, 48 g protein

Keto Roast Beef

Makes 4 to 6 servings

1 (2-pound) beef rump roast

4 cups Beef Bone Broth (see page 25) or Chicken Bone Broth (see page 24)

½ cup canned coconut milk (do not use "lite" coconut milk)

7 garlic cloves, minced

2 cups sliced mushrooms

OPTIONAL

2 large onions, chopped

½ cup sliced celery

Salt and pepper, to taste

½ teaspoon sweet paprika

Roast beef is one of those foods that reminds me of the Sunday dinners and holiday meals of my childhood. Now that I am an adult, I have roast beef whenever I want. I simply start this slow cooker recipe in the morning before work and come home to a hot meal—or a component that can be used for future sandwiches, bowls, tacos, and more.

1. Add the broth, coconut milk, garlic, mushrooms, and optional ingredients to a slow cooker. Stir once.

2. Nestle the meat into the slow cooker.

3. Put the lid on the slow cooker and turn it to a low setting for 6 to 8 hours, or on high for 4 to 6 hours.

Macros per 1 cup serving (made with optional ingredients): 384 calories, 1.4 g net carbs, 2.1 g total carbs, 0.7 g fiber, 1 g sugars, 26.7 g total fat, 32.4 g protein

Seasoned Ground Beef

Makes 8 servings

1 tablespoon butter

2 pounds ground beef

2 teaspoons garlic powder

1 teaspoon cumin or paprika

Salt and pepper, to taste

It is a great convenience to have a couple of pounds of seasoned, precooked ground beef on hand to make a quick taco or keto bowl, top some zucchini noodles, stuff into a wrap, or season a salad. It's all good! Feel free to switch out half the ground beef with ground pork, lamb, or any other meat you'd like to use.

1. Melt the butter in a large skillet over medium-high heat.

2. Add the beef, garlic powder, and cumin, salt, and pepper and cook until the beef is medium/medium-well done. Be careful not to overcook the beef if you plan to use it for another hot meal that involves more cooking time.

3. Turn off the heat and allow the meat to cool in the pan. Transfer portions into single-serving or small covered containers or freezer bags and store them for up to 4 days in the refrigerator, or up to 3 months in the freezer.

Macros per serving: 385 calories, 0 g net carbs, 0 g total carbs, 0 g fiber, 0 g sugars, 35 g total fat, 17 g protein

Coconut Keto Baked Fish

Makes 4 (8-ounce) servings or 8 (4-ounce) servings

¼ cup liquid coconut oil (plus extra to grease the pan)

4 teaspoons fresh lemon juice

2 pounds cod or other thick fish, fillets or steaks

½ cup canned coconut milk (do not use "lite" coconut milk)

Salt, to taste

OPTIONAL

black pepper, to taste

1 teaspoon onion salt

1 teaspoon garlic salt

½ teaspoon ground ginger

2 teaspoons ground coriander

1 teaspoon ground cumin

¼ teaspoon cayenne

¼ teaspoon ground black pepper

¼ teaspoon ground turmeric

¼ cup chopped fresh chives, parsley, or cilantro, for garnish

I've offered a version of this incredibly versatile recipe in almost every cookbook I've written. In this recipe, you can use a mild white fish, such as cod, or opt for salmon or tuna, if you prefer something meatier.

1. Lightly grease a baking dish with some of the coconut oil. Make sure the dish is large enough to fit all of the fish in a single layer.

2. In a small bowl, whisk together the lemon juice, ¼ cup coconut oil, coconut milk, salt, and optional spices. Set the bowl aside.

3. Cut the fillets crosswise into 2-inch-wide strips and place in the baking dish. Pour the lemon juice mixture over fish, making sure to coat it evenly. Cover the baking dish and refrigerate for 1 hour.

4. Preheat the oven to 350°F. Remove the fish from the refrigerator. Uncover the baking dish and bake the fish for 10 minutes.

5. Check the fish and spoon any drippings over the top. Cover the dish tightly with foil and return it to the oven for 15 minutes, or until the fish is opaque or until a food thermometer reads 145°F.

6. If you like, garnish the fish with chopped herbs, such as chives.

NOTE You'll notice that the portion sizes in this recipe are large, allowing 8 ounces of fish per person. If you'd prefer a more average portion, serve 4-ounce portions (in which case, you'll end up with 8 servings).

Macros per 8-ounce serving (made with cod and optional ingredients):
278 calories, 1.1 g net carbs, 1.8 g total carbs, 0.7 g fiber, 1.2 g sugars, 21.8 g total fat, 20.8 g protein

4 | EARLY-DAY KETO MEALS

BREAKFAST IS TRULY THE EASIEST MEAL OF THE DAY TO "DO KETO."

Eggs, bacon, sausage, full-fat yogurt . . . they are all easy, keto-compliant breakfast foods. However, if you're looking for something a little fancier than a hard-boiled egg and a cup of coffee, here are some delightful, early-day keto meals to enjoy!

Breakfast Taco

Makes 6 servings

2 egg whites

Pinch of cream of tartar

Dash of cumin or chile powder

½ tablespoon avocado oil, coconut oil, or lard

1 pound bulk Mexican chorizo or other sausage of your choice (breakfast, Italian, etc.)

OPTIONAL

1 garlic clove, minced

Salt and pepper

Tacos, a lunchtime favorite from my childhood in Northern California, often wind up in my kids' lunchboxes.

1. To make the tortillas: In the bowl of a stand mixter, whisk together the egg whites, cream of tartar, and cumin or chile powder until the mixture is light yellow in color. Set it aside.

2. Add the oil to a large nonstick skillet over medium heat. Heat for 1 minute. Pour 2 tablespoons of the tortilla batter into the pan, rotating the pan to help distribute the batter.

3. Cover the pan and cook the tortilla for 2 minutes. Flip the tortilla, cover the pan, and cook for 2 more minutes.

4. Remove the tortilla and set it on a plate. Fold the tortilla in half so it resembles a taco shell and allow it to cool.

5. Repeat the steps with the remaining batter, then wipe down the skillet.

6. To make the taco filling: Cook the meat in the skillet over medium-high heat and, if you choose to use it, add the garlic, salt, and pepper. Sauté the meat until it is fully cooked through.

8. Assemble the tacos by holding the tortilla with one hand and using the other hand to fill the tortilla with taco meat.

Macros per serving (made with chorizo): 210 calories, 2.7 g net carbs, 2.7 g total carbs, 0 g fiber, 0.1 g sugars, 20.7 g total fat, 15.4 g protein

Cup o' Eggs

Makes 1 serving

---

2 large eggs

1 tablespoon heavy cream,
half-and-half, milk,
coconut cream,
or coconut milk

Salt and pepper, to taste

OPTIONAL

1 tablespoon chopped
and cooked low-carb
vegetables, such as
broccoli or mushrooms

1 tablespoon shredded
cheese of your choice

1 tablespoon chopped or
shredded cooked meat,
poultry, fish, or deli meat
of your choice

Egg cups are a keto favorite. They are easy, versatile, and serve as a great base for small amounts of leftover raw or cooked ingredients. For this recipe you'll need a small ovenproof cup, such as a ramekin.

1. Preheat the oven to 350°F.

2. In a large bowl, whisk together the eggs and cream. Season the mixture with salt and pepper, to taste.

3. Add any optional ingredients you would like to use. Stir to combine.

4. Pour the egg mixture into a greased ramekin or ovenproof cup.

5. Bake the eggs for 15 to 20 minutes, depending upon how you like them.

Macros per serving (made with heavy cream, 1 tablespoon cooked broccoli, 1 tablespoon cheddar, and 1 tablespoon cooked ham): 250 calories, 1.7 g net carbs, 2.7 g total carbs, 1 g fiber, 0.9 g sugars, 18.9 g fat, 16.5 g protein

Keto Hash

Makes 4 servings

1 pound bulk breakfast sausage (or Italian sausage or Mexican chorizo, casings removed)

2 garlic cloves, minced

1 bunch radishes, diced

2 small zucchini, diced

OPTIONAL

Salt and pepper, to taste

While hash is strongly associated with high-carbohydrate potatoes, there are plenty of low-carb veggies that make a delicious, keto-compliant hash! If you're an egg lover, feel free to serve this hash with a fried egg on top!

1. Place a large skillet over medium-high heat. Add the sausage, breaking up the meat with a spoon. Add the garlic and cook until it is fragrant but not yet brown.

2. Stir in the radishes and cook them for 3 or 4 minutes, or until the vegetables have softened.

3. Add the zucchini and, if you like, salt and pepper, to taste. Stir the mixture to evenly distribute all the ingredients and cook until the zucchini is just softened, about 5 minutes.

4. Remove the skillet from heat. Transfer the hash to 4 plates.

Macros per serving (made with breakfast sausage and optional ingredients): 532 calories, 3.7 g net carbs, 5 g total carbs, 1.3 g fiber, 1.25 g sugars, 43.5 g fat, 28.3 g protein

Keto Omelet

Makes 1 serving

2 large eggs

1 tablespoon heavy cream, milk, coconut cream, or coconut milk

Salt and pepper

1 tablespoon butter or oil of your choice, for the skillet

OPTIONAL

1 to 2 tablespoons chopped meat, cheese, herbs, etc., at room temperature

An omelet is one of those staples that everyone should know how to make. This recipe makes a basic keto omelet that can be dressed up with cheese, meat, chopped cooked veggies, or anything else that might be hanging out in your fridge.

1. In a large bowl, whisk together the eggs and cream. Season the mix with salt and pepper, to taste. Set the bowl aside.

2. Melt the butter or add the oil to a medium skillet, over medium-high heat.

3. Pour the egg mixture into the skillet and allow it to cook, undisturbed, until the eggs look wobbly. If you're adding optional ingredients, such as meat, cheese, or herbs, sprinkle them onto the surface of the egg.

4. Before the egg fully sets, use a thin metal spatula to lift up one side of the omelet, and fold it toward the middle of the omelet. Repeat with the other side of the omelet.

5. To serve, quickly slide the omelet onto a plate.

Macros per serving (made with butter, heavy cream, and no optional ingredients): 228 calories, 1.2 g net carbs, 1.2 g total carbs, 0 g fiber, 0.8 g sugars, 19.3 g fat, 12.9 g protein

Keto Egg Casserole

Makes 6 servings

8 large eggs

½ cup heavy cream or coconut cream

Butter or oil, to grease the baking pan

½ pound bulk pork breakfast sausage (or bulk Italian sausage, Mexican chorizo, or ground beef), cooked and drained

½ cup shredded Pepper Jack cheese

OPTIONAL

Salt and pepper, to taste

This is one of those homey brunch casseroles that regularly shows up in church cookbooks and women's magazines—and for good reason. An egg casserole is easy to make, economical, and serves a crowd. Feel free to modify the meat (you can use 8 ounces of whatever cooked meat you have in the fridge—even crumbled bacon!) or add a few tablespoons of cooked chopped veggies or herbs, or replace the Pepper Jack called for with any type of cheese you have on hand.

1. Preheat the oven to 350°F.

2. In a large bowl, whisk together the eggs, cream, and optional salt and pepper. Set the bowl aside.

3. Grease a 9 × 13-inch baking dish with softened butter or oil of your choice.

4. Pour half the egg mixture into the dish.

5. Sprinkle the sausage over the egg mixture.

6. Pour the remaining egg mixture into the dish and sprinkle the shredded cheese over the top. Place the pan in the oven.

7. Cook the casserole for 20 to 25 minutes, or until the edges begin to turn golden and the casserole has started to set (you want it to be a bit soft when you take it out of the oven, so that the casserole doesn't overcook).

Macros per serving (made with heavy cream, breakfast sausage, and optional ingredients): 350 calories, 1.5 g net carbs, 1.5 g total carbs, 0 g fiber, 0.5 g sugars, 28.7 g fat, 22.6 g protein

Baked Avocado

Makes 2 servings

1 Hass avocado, peeled, pitted, and halved

1 slice Make-Ahead Bacon (see page 16) (or 1 link cooked breakfast sausage, ¼ cup cooked ham, chicken, or other meat, chopped)

2 large eggs

Salt and pepper, to taste

If you have never baked an avocado, you are in for a treat! Feel free to change things up by replacing the bacon or sausage for small amounts (no more than ¼ cup) of leftover chopped veggies, cheese, herbs, or meat.

1. Arrange rack in the middle of oven and preheat the oven to 425°F.

2. Using a cookie scoop, melon baller, or small spoon, gently enlarge the indentation in the avocado left by the pit. Place the scooped-out avocado flesh in a small freezer-safe container and freeze it for later use. Arrange the prepared avocado halves on a baking pan or in a muffin tin, cradling each avocado half into a cup.

3. Sprinkle half the bacon, or other meat, into the indentation of each avocado half.

4. Crack 1 egg in a small bowl. Gently pour the whole egg into the avocado indentation, on top of the crumbled bacon or other filling, being careful not to break the yolk. Repeat this step with the second egg and the other avocado half.

5. Season the eggs with salt and pepper.

6. Gently arrange the remaining bacon or other filling on top of the egg, again being careful not to break the yolk.

7. Bake the avocado halves for 13 to 15 minutes, depending on how you like your eggs.

8. Remove the pan from the oven and serve immediately.

Macros per serving (made with 1 slice bacon): 328 calories, 2.5 g net carbs, 9.2 g total carbs, 6.7 g fiber, 0.9 g sugars, 28.5 g fat, 11.7 g protein

5 Grab-and-Go Keto Non-Egg Breakfast Options

In the world of keto, eggs are considered a near-perfect food: They're high in fat, with a good amount of protein and without a single gram of carbohydrates, they are convenient, versatile, and nutritious. But a person can eat only so many eggs before growing tired of them. If you are one of the many keto eaters who is "all egged out" but unsure of what to use as an easy egg alternative, have no fear. Here are five easy egg-free breakfast options:

* A single-serve carton of unflavored whole milk or container of plain Greek yogurt

* A cup of black coffee blended with a scoop of keto protein powder and a splash of dairy or coconut cream

* Three or 4 slices Make-Ahead Bacon (see page 16) or a few precooked breakfast sausage links tucked, taco-style, into a large lettuce leaf and dressed with a splash of hot sauce

* Two cooked breakfast sausage patties with a dollop of guacamole (or a few Hass avocado slices) in between (the patties become the "bun")

* Any of the smoothies on pages 64–66.

* Any of the fat bombs on pages 100–115.

Keto Rich Coconut Porridge

Makes 1 serving

1 large egg, beaten

1 tablespoon coconut flour

¼ teaspoon ground psyllium husk powder

2 tablespoons butter or coconut oil

4 tablespoons coconut cream

OPTIONAL

Pinch of salt

This popular recipe uses coconut flour and psyllium to create a warm, comforting cereal. Feel free to double the recipe so you can share it!

1. In a small bowl, whisk together the egg, coconut flour, psyllium husk powder, and optional salt. Set aside.

2. Melt the butter and coconut cream in a small saucepan over medium-low heat.

3. Slowly whisk the egg-coconut flour mixture into the pan and continue to whisk until the texture is thick and smooth.

4. Remove the pan from the heat and enjoy the cereal while it's warm.

Macros per serving (made with butter and optional ingredient: 350 calories, 4 g net carbs, 9 g total carbs, 5 g fiber, 0.5 g sugars, 49 g fat, 9 g protein

Keto Pancakes

Makes 2 servings, or 4 to 6 pancakes

4 ounces cream cheese, at room temperature

4 eggs, lightly beaten

2 tablespoons coconut flour

4 to 6 pats of butter or 1 tablespoon coconut oil, to grease the skillet

OPTIONAL

1 teaspoon ground cinnamon or a spice blend, such as pumpkin pie spice or apple pie spice blend

This recipe is easily doubled or tripled if you're cooking for a crowd. Any unused pancakes can be stored in the fridge for up to 3 days or saved in freezer wrap and frozen for up to three months.

1. Add the cream cheese, eggs, coconut flour, and any spice you choose to use to the bowl of stand mixer fitted with the paddle attachment. Mix on medium-low speed until all the ingredients are blended and the batter is smooth.

2. Add a pat of the butter or coconut oil to a large skillet over medium-high heat. When the fat has melted, pour about 2 tablespoons of the batter onto the skillet to form a pancake. (It is easier to make each pancake at a time, so that the individual pancake batter doesn't run together.) It will be a bit thinner than a traditional pancake, but it will cook in a similar way. When the pancake batter begins to bubble, it is ready to flip.

3. Flip the pancake and cook until the bottom is golden, about 2 minutes. Place the pancake on a plate, cover with a clean dishtowel, and set aside. Repeat until all the batter has been used.

4. To serve, divide the pancakes between two plates and either eat them as they are or dress them up with nut butter, whipped cream, or another topping of your choice.

Macros per serving (2 pancakes with no topping): 365 calories, 5 g net carbs, 8 g total carbs, 3 g fiber, 1 g sugars, 19 g fat, 17 g protein

5 | KETO SIPS AND SLURPS

HOW MUCH THOUGHT DO YOU GIVE TO THE BEVERAGES YOU consume? If you're like most of us, probably not much. But one wrong drink can completely wipe out your day's macros! Fortunately, it's easy to make many delicious keto-compliant drinks. You'll find some of my favorites in this chapter.

Fatty Iced Tea

Makes 2 servings

- 2 to 4 black, green, or white tea bags
- 3 cups boiling water
- 2 tablespoons unsalted butter
- 2 tablespoons coconut oil
- ¼ cup heavy cream, coconut milk, or coconut cream

Making your own iced tea, rather than buying a commercial product, is fun, economical, quick, easy—and you know exactly what you're getting.

1. Place the tea bags in a saucepan or a heatproof bowl and pour the boiling water over the tea bags. Let them steep in the water for 2 to 4 minutes, depending on how strong you like your tea.

2. Remove the tea bags from the pan or bowl.

3. Add the butter and coconut oil to the tea and whisk to blend.

4. Place the tea mixture in the fridge to cool.

5. Add the heavy cream or coconut milk to the cooled tea and serve.

Macros per 1½-cup serving (made with heavy cream): 180 calories, 0.4 g net carbs, 0.4 g total carbs, 0 g fiber, 0 g sugars, 19.4 g fat, 1.6 g protein

Keto Chai Latte

Makes 2 servings

2 to 3 cups water

2 or 3 chai tea bags (use 3 if you like a stronger-tasting beverage)

½ tablespoon coconut oil

1 cup coconut milk

Chai latte is one of my favorite warm drinks. While traditional chai tea is made with black tea and whole spices, you can use chai tea bags to make a quicker cup of tea that tastes just as delicious.

1. Add water to a small saucepan over medium heat until the water boils.

2. Turn the heat to the low, add the tea bags, and allow them to steep for 10 minutes.

3. Remove the tea bags and whisk in the coconut oil and coconut milk.

Macros per 1- to 1½-cup serving: 321 calories, 4.5 g net carbs, 8 g total carbs, 3.5 g fiber, 4 g sugars, 33.1 g fat, 2.8 g protein

Bulletproof Coffee

Makes 2 servings

2 cups warm coffee of your choice, brewed as you would normally brew it

2 tablespoons unsalted butter, preferably grass-fed

2 tablespoons coconut oil

OPTIONAL

1 or more tablespoons coconut cream or heavy whipping cream

1 teaspoon vanilla extract

"Bulletproof coffee" is blended with fat. This lovely version can be made at home, taken to work in a thermos, and then warmed in the kitchen for a late-morning or early-afternoon treat.

Add all the ingredients to a blender. Process until the mixture is smooth and frothy.

Macros per 1-cup serving (made with 1 tablespoon coconut cream): 248 calories, 4 g net carbs, 4 g total carbs, 0 g fiber, 3.9 g sugars, 26.4 g fat, 0.5 g protein

Bulletproof Drink Drops

Makes 9 drops

½ cup ghee (see page 62)

1 cup coconut oil, melted

¼ teaspoon sea salt

OPTIONAL

½ teaspoon cinnamon powder

TIP To make Bulletproof Coffee using Bulletproof Drink Drops: Place one cube and 10 ounces of hot black coffee in a blender. Process the mixture until it is well combined and foamy.

Although these fat drops are not a beverage per se, they can be kept in your freezer and dropped into a cup of hot coffee, hot tea, or hot chocolate—or even tossed into a blender to enhance a smoothie—instantly transforming any low-carb beverage into a fatty keto drink.

1. Combine all the ingredients in small bowl.

2. Whisk and then pour the mixture into nine ice cube tray depressions, filling them to the top.

3. Place the tray in the freezer.

4. Once the drops have set, pop them from the tray into a glass container and cover it. Store the drops in the freezer for up to three months until you are ready to use them.

Macros per serving (made with optional cinnamon): 309 calories, 0.1 g net carbs, 0.2 g total carbs, 0.1 g fiber, 0 g sugars, 35.5 g fat, 2.8 g protein

All about Ghee . . . and How to Make It

Ghee is clarified butter that does not contain milk solids and water. To make your own ghee, melt one pound of unsalted organic butter in a small saucepan over medium heat. When the butter has melted, reduce the heat to medium-low and let it simmer for 10 to 12 minutes. Remove the pan from the heat and skim the foam off the top of the melted butter. Return the pan to the heat and bring the butter to a simmer once again. The butter will be golden, more foam will appear on top, and dark milk solids may develop on the bottom of the pan. After 10 to 12 minutes, skim the foam, turn off the heat, take the pan off the stove, and let the pan cool for 3 minutes. Pour the butter through a fine sieve or strainer into a clean glass jar with a tight-fitting lid. You can store the ghee at room temperature for up to 1 month, although I prefer to keep ghee in the fridge, where it can stay for up to 3 months.

Iced Coconut Coffee

Makes 2 servings

12 ounces (about 1.5 cups)
prepared coffee of your
choice, cooled

2 tablespoons coconut oil

2 tablespoons heavy cream
or coconut cream

**Coconut and coffee are a delicious pairing, as you'll discover
when you sip this invigorating iced java drink.**

Add all ingredients to a blender. Process the mixture until
it is smooth and frothy.

Macros per 6-ounce serving (made with heavy cream): 180 calories, 0.4 g net carbs,
0.4 g total carbs, 0 g fiber, 0 g sugars, 19.4 g fat, 1.6 g protein

Hot Fatty Cocoa

Makes 1 serving

1 cup coconut milk

2 tablespoons unsalted
butter

½ tablespoon coconut oil

1 tablespoon unsweetened
cocoa powder (Dutch or
regular)

OPTIONAL

Drop of vanilla or
peppermint extract

Liquid or powdered
stevia, to taste

**Did you know that cocoa can be keto? It's true! This high-fat,
low-carb version is the perfect treat for a winter evening.**

1. Warm the coconut milk, butter, and coconut oil in a small
saucepan over medium heat until the mixture begins to
simmer.

2. Pour the liquid into a blender and add the cocoa powder
and vanilla or peppermint extract. Process the mixture until
it is blended and frothy.

3. If you like, add stevia, to taste.

Macros per serving (made with optional ingredients): 800 calories, 5 g net carbs,
12 g total carbs, 7 g fiber, 7 g sugars, 80 g fat, 6.8 g protein

Coffee Coconut Smoothie

Makes 1 serving

6 ounces (about ¾ cup) prepared black coffee, cold

½ cup full-fat canned coconut milk or coconut cream

¼ medium Hass avocado

1 tablespoon coconut oil

OPTIONAL

Liquid or powdered stevia, to taste

If you miss milkshakes, give this thick, creamy drink a try. It uses all the good fat of a traditional milkshake, while omitting the sugary carbs and adding an enjoyable jolt from the coffee.

Place all the ingredients in a blender and process until the mixture is smooth. If you prefer a thinner shake, add a few tablespoons of cold water or more coffee.

Macros per serving (made with full-fat coconut milk and without optional sweetener): 342 calories, 3.2 g net carbs, 3.2 g total carbs, 0 g fiber, 0 g sugar, 37.7 g fat, 2.5 g protein

Keto-Compliant Green Drink

Makes 2 servings

1 cup coconut milk

2 cups water (more if you prefer a thinner consistency)

1 cup loosely packed baby spinach

½ medium Hass avocado

Juice of 1 lemon or lime, about 2 tablespoons

NOTE This recipe doesn't store well, but it can be halved, if you can't find anyone to share it with you.

Smoothies are not always the best choices for keto eaters, because, typically, they are chock-full of simple carbs. This green drink—made in a blender—is different. Don't expect a fruity, sweet drink. Instead, the result is an herbaceous, decidedly green-tasting smoothie—and you will feel so amazing after drinking it!

Add all the ingredients to a blender and puree the mixture until it is smooth.

Macros per 1½-cup serving: 380 calories, 5.5 g net carbs, 12.5 g total carbs, 7 g fiber, 4.7 g sugars, 38 g fat, 4.2 g protein

Low-Carb Purple Smoothie

Makes 2 servings

½ cup frozen raspberries

¼ cup frozen blackberries

½ cup plain whole-milk Greek yogurt

Liquid or powdered stevia, to taste

1 cup unsweetened coconut milk

OPTIONAL

Water, added teaspoon by teaspoon, if you'd like a thinner beverage

If you miss fruit, this smoothie is for you. The recipe contains frozen raspberries and blackberries. If you're watching your macros, be aware that this is a two-serving recipe, so remember to limit yourself to half the smoothie. You can freeze the other half in an ice cube tray and blend it with water at a later time if no one is available to share this delicious drink with you.

Add all the ingredients to a blender and puree the mixture until it is smooth.

Macros per 1¼ cup serving: 465 calories, 6 g net carbs, 20 g total carbs, 14 g fiber, 19 g sugars, 28.9 g fat, 33.4 g protein

Spicy Keto Mocktail

Makes 4 generous servings

Juice of 1 lemon or lime (about 2 tablespoons)

1 (2-inch) section of ginger, peeled

1 cup cold still water (either bottled or from the tap)

1 liter cold sparkling water, such as mineral water, seltzer, or soda water

OPTIONAL

Ice cubes or crushed ice for the pitcher or individual glasses

It's no fun to watch everyone else enjoy a fancy cocktail when you're abstaining from alcohol. This bright-tasting mocktail will make going booze-free a lot easier.

1. Add the lemon or lime juice, ginger, and water to a blender. Process the mixture until it is smooth.

2. Pour the mixture into a large pitcher. Add the sparkling water to the pitcher and stir to combine all the ingredients.

3. To serve, pour the drink into chilled glasses and enjoy.

Macros per ¾-cup serving (using lemon juice): 6 calories, 1.4 g net carbs, 1.5 g total carbs, 1.5 g sugar, 0.1 g fiber, 0 g fat, 0.1 g protein

Salty Keto Water

Makes 1 serving

½ teaspoon pink Himalayan
salt

8 ounces water

This recipe isn't as "sexy" as some of the others in this book, but Salty Keto Water is a popular keto way to help reach ketosis.

Add the salt to a glass of water. Vigorously stir the water until the salt dissolves and then drink it.

Electrolyte Sipper

Makes 1 liter

5 cups water

2 tablespoons lemon
or lime juice

½ teaspoon potassium
chloride or lite salt (a
mixture of sodium and
potassium chloride)

¼ teaspoon pink Himalayan
salt

2 teaspoons powdered
Magnesium Calm (or
another powdered
magnesium) supplement

OPTIONAL

Powdered or liquid stevia,
to taste

You can sip this recipe throughout the day.

1. Pour the water into a large pitcher or carafe.

2. Stir in all the remaining ingredients until well combined. Alternately, you can combine all the ingredients in a blender and then transfer the mixture to a pitcher or carafe. This beverage does not need to be refrigerated if you drink it within an 8-hour period.

6

SMALL
PLATES
AND QUICK
BITES:
LUNCHES
AND OTHER
SMALL
MEALS

WHEN YOU THINK OF STANDARD MIDDAY FARE, OFFERINGS SUCH AS

sandwiches, wraps, and paninis usually spring to mind. While

all of these are fast, convenient, economical, and delicious, not

a single one is keto compliant. In this chapter, you'll discover a

wide range of delicious, high-fat, low-carb foods that will keep

you on track, whether you enjoy them at home or pack them

for lunch to eat at school or work.

Shrimp Avocado Salad

Makes 2 servings

Juice of 1 lime

2 tablespoons extra-virgin olive oil

1 pound large or jumbo cooked shrimp (16 to 24 count), peeled and cleaned

4 cups baby spinach

1 Hass avocado, diced

OPTIONAL

Salt and pepper, to taste

Shrimp and avocado beautifully pair protein and fat, making them a great combo for keto eaters. This luxurious lunch salad travels well and can be customized with the addition of extra veggies.

1. In a small bowl, whisk together the lime juice, olive oil, and optional salt and pepper.

2. Chop the shrimp or leave it whole (I like to chop it, so I get a bit in each bite of salad).

3. Place the shrimp in a large bowl. Add the baby spinach and avocado to the bowl. Drizzle the lime juice mixture over the top and toss to combine. If desired, add additional salt and pepper, to taste.

Macros per serving (made with optional ingredient): 595 calories, 4.1 g net carbs, 15 g total carbs, 10.9 g fiber, 0.9 g sugars, 36.1 g total fat, 53.5 g protein

Grab-and-Go Almost Cobb Salad

Makes 2 servings

2 to 3 tablespoons of your favorite salad dressing (see page 26 for Keto Vinaigrette)

4 cups chopped romaine lettuce

1 medium Hass avocado, diced

½ cup cubed cheddar cheese

2 large Perfect Hard-Boiled Eggs (see page 20), roughly chopped

OPTIONAL

2 or 3 slices Make-Ahead Bacon (see page 16), crumbled

The Cobb salad has been a protein lover's favorite since it was first created in the 1930s. This keto-compliant version is streamlined and features only five ingredients. It travels well, making it a great option for picnics and brown bag lunches.

1. If you are serving the salad in bowls, in a medium bowl, gently toss all the ingredients and divide them between 2 individual bowls.

2. If you are packing the salad, pour half the dressing into the bottom of two lunch containers. Divide the lettuce into two portions and set them aside.

3. Add half the diced avocado to the containers.

4. Place half the cheese, half the chopped egg, and half the lettuce on top of the avocado in the lunch containers and top them with the crumbled bacon, if you are using it.

5. Seal the containers immediately and store them in the fridge.

6. Before eating, gently shake the container to distribute the dressing.

Macros per serving (made without optional ingredient): 470 calories, 2.4 g net carbs, 8.3 g total carbs, 5.9 g fiber, 1 g sugars, 43.1 g total fat, 16.2 g protein

Chunky Cauliflower Salad

Makes 2 servings

4 cups small cauliflower florets

¼ cup Keto Vinaigrette (see page 26)

4 slices Make-Ahead Bacon (see page 16), crumbled

½ cup chopped black olives

OPTIONAL

Salt and pepper, to taste

1 or 2 tablespoons minced chives or parsley

Most of us think of leafy greens when we hear the word "salad." This fun, sturdy salad, however, is based not on lettuce but cauliflower.

1. Add an inch of water to a large pot fitted with a steamer basket. Place the cauliflower in the steamer. Set the pot over medium-high heat and cook the cauliflower until it is barely fork-tender. Time will vary depending on your cauliflower, but this typically will be between 5 and 8 minutes..

2. When the cauliflower is done, place it in a large bowl, and toss it with the salad dressing while it is still warm.

3. Allow the cauliflower to cool to room temperature. Once it is cool, gently mix in the bacon and olives. Add salt and pepper to taste, if you like, as well as the optional minced chives or parsley.

Macros per serving (made with optional ingredients): 288 calories, 4.5 g net carbs, 10 g total carbs, 5.5 g fiber, 3.8 g sugars, 31 g total fat, 18 g protein

The Keto Grab-and-Go
SALAD BLUEPRINT

Makes 1 serving

3 tablespoons Keto Vinaigrette (see page 26) or your favorite salad dressing

1 Hass avocado, chopped

3 cups baby spinach, chopped romaine lettuce, or another salad green

1 cup cooked (or canned) fish, seafood, poultry, or red meat of your choice

½ cup chopped cooked or raw vegetables, including riced cauliflower or broccoli stems

OPTIONAL

Salt and pepper, to taste

½ tablespoon or more chopped fresh herbs of your choice

½ cup shredded or cubed cheese

1 Perfect Hard-Boiled Egg (see page 20), chopped

1 or 2 slices Make-Ahead Bacon (see page 16), chopped

½ cup or more shredded unsweetened coconut

If you read cooking magazines or watch any of the cooking channels on YouTube, you have no doubt seen recipes for "grab-and-go" salads, which are often made (and transported to school or work) in Mason jars for an easy, delicious keto-compliant lunch (and they are perfect for picnics). You can make a grab-and-go salad with about anything you have in your kitchen—even if you have only small amounts of this and that. Just layer the ingredients into a Mason jar or any other "grab-and-go" container, toss it in your bag, and you've got an easy lunch (or breakfast or dinner for that matter). Listed here are just a few ingredients you might consider using.

1. Add the vinaigrette or salad dressing and the optional salt and pepper to a lunch container or Mason jar, and gently shake it until the ingredients are well combined.

2. Add the avocado to the dressing in the jar or container and toss gently until the avocado is well coated. Adjust seasonings to taste.

3. Add the spinach, cooked fish, vegetables, and any of the other ingredients you'd like to use. Do not stir! Allow the dressing and avocado to sit at the bottom of the container until you are ready to eat.

4. Place the lid on the container and store it in the refrigerator.

5. Before eating, gently turn the container upside down a few times to distribute the dressing.

Macros per serving depend upon what ingredients you use.

Salmon Chowder

Makes 4 large servings

2 tablespoons butter

6 cups Chicken Bone Broth (see recipe for chicken bone broth, page 24)

1 teaspoon garlic powder

1 pound frozen salmon fillets or pieces, thawed and cut into bite-size pieces

OPTIONAL

1 teaspoon onion powder

½ teaspoon dried thyme leaves

1 teaspoon fresh chopped dill or ½ teaspoon dried dill

1 teaspoon fresh chopped parsley or ½ teaspoon dried parsley

Salt and pepper, to taste

1 (15-ounce) can coconut milk or half-and-half (about 1¾ cup)

A good bowl of chowder brightens even the dreariest day. This version is made with salmon. Feel free to substitute about 16 ounces of canned salmon, if that's what you have on hand.

1. Heat the butter in a large saucepan over medium-low heat.

2. Whisk in the chicken broth, garlic powder, and optional spices. Simmer the broth for about 15 minutes. Season to taste with salt and pepper.

3. Add the salmon and coconut milk or half-and-half to the pan. Bring the stock to a gentle simmer and cook just until the fish is firm and tender. Serve immediately.

Macros per serving (made with coconut milk and optional ingredients): 850 calories, 4.4 g net carbs, 7 g total carbs, 2.6 g fiber, 5 g sugars, 57 g total fat, 77 g protein

Creamy Keto Bisque

Makes 4 servings

5 tablespoons butter

1 medium head cauliflower, chopped

Salt and freshly ground black pepper to taste

8 cups Chicken Bone Broth (see page 24)

1 cup heavy cream

OPTIONAL

½ teaspoon garlic powder

1 teaspoon onion powder

½ to 1 tablespoon minced chives, for garnish

Cauliflower soup is one of my absolute favorite soups. This creamy version is deeply satisfying and comforting. I strongly recommend that you use the optional flavorings and feel free to experiment with your favorite spices or fresh herbs.

1. Add the 5 tablespoons of butter to a large soup pot and place it over medium heat. Add the cauliflower, season with salt and pepper and optional seasonings, and sauté for about 10 minutes, or until the cauliflower has softened.

2. Stir in the broth and raise the heat to medium-high.

3. Bring the mixture to a boil, and then reduce the heat to medium-low. Cover the pot and simmer the soup for 45 minutes.

4. Remove the soup from heat. Blend the soup with an immersion blender or hand-held mixer. Adjust the seasonings. Mix the cream into the pot and continue blending until the soup is smooth.

5. Add optional chives for garnish and serve.

6. Place in an airtight container and store for up to five days in the fridge, or freeze for up to three months.

Macros per 2-cup serving (made with optional ingredients): 360 calories, 4.7 g net carbs, 10 g total carbs, 5.3 g fiber, 5.5 g sugars, 28.5 g total fat, 4.6 g protein

Fatabulous Cream Soup
BLUEPRINT

Yield varies

3 tablespoons fat of choice, such as avocado oil, bacon grease, butter, coconut oil, ghee, lard, or extra-virgin olive oil

½ cup chopped celery and/or zucchini and/or broccoli and/or cauliflower

2 cups Chicken Bone Broth (see page 24), Beef Bone Broth (see page 25), or another type of broth

1 cup heavy cream or coconut cream

OPTIONAL

Salt and pepper, to taste

1 to 3 teaspoons garlic powder

¼ to 1 teaspoon cumin, paprika, basil, oregano, or a combination of spices

1 to 3 tablespoons chopped fresh herbs of your choice

for a chunky, meaty soup: 1 to 3 cups chopped cooked seafood, poultry, or meat

Soup is one of those foods that a lot of people make without a recipe. If you're one of them, you probably know what ingredients to use and even in what order to add the ingredients to make a great soup. If you have never cooked recipe-free (or made a ketogenic soup without a recipe), this blueprint will help you create a delicious, creamy keto-compliant soup. You can change the ingredients depending upon what you are in the mood for and what's on hand. Have fun!

1. Add the fat to a large soup pot or saucepan and set it over medium heat. Add the vegetables of your choice and sauté them until they're soft. **NOTE**: The time this will take depends on the vegetables you use, but two to eight minutes is a good average.

2. Add the broth and simmer the mixture for 15 to 20 minutes.

3. If you want a smooth soup: Allow the soup to cool and then transfer it to a blender. Puree the soup until it is smooth and then return it to the soup pot. Or, leave soup in the pot and puree over the stove using an immersion blender.

3. Stir in the cream and the optional seasonings, herbs, and seafood, poultry, or meat, depending on your preference. Adjust the seasonings and cook the soup for 5 to 10 minutes to blend flavors.

Macros per serving: Calorie, fat, protein, and carb counts will vary with what you decide to use to make your cream soup.

Greek Goddess Keto Wrap

Makes 1 serving

2 tablespoons full-fat unflavored Greek yogurt

2 tablespoons crumbled feta

2 tablespoons pitted, chopped Kalamata or other olives

¼ Hass avocado, diced

2 large chard leaves

OPTIONAL

Salt and pepper

2 teaspoons minced fresh dill

This glorious, veggie-heavy wrap is a wonderful change of pace from all the meat most keto wraps contain.

1. In a large bowl, mash the yogurt, feta, olives, and avocado into a chunky paste. Season the mixture with optional ingredients, if desired. Set the bowl aside.

2. Place the chard leaves on a flat surface. Using a pair of kitchen shears or a knife, remove the stems and about two inches of the spine from each leaf. (You can either discard them or chop and sauté them to use in another dish.)

3. Divide the feta mixture in half and spoon a horizontal mound on the lower third of each leaf, just above the area where you've removed the spine.

4. To make the wrap, fold in the two vertical ends of one leaf, as if you were rolling up a burrito.

5. Begin rolling the leaf from the bottom.

6. If necessary, use a toothpick to keep the wrap together.

7. Repeat with second leaf and serve.

Macros per serving (made with optional ingredients): 275 calories, 4.9 g net carbs, 11 g total carbs, 6.1 g fiber, 2 g sugars, 23 g total fat, 8.6 g protein

KETO WRAPPERS

Here are two easy wrapper recipes to play with. Fill them with whatever keto-friendly fillings you'd like, from deli meat to tuna salad to pulled pork.

Bouncy Wrapper

Makes about 5 (8-inch) wraps

¼ cup coconut flour

3 large eggs

¾ cup milk of choice (dairy, nut milk, coconut milk, etc.)

Salt and pepper, to taste

1 teaspoon coconut oil

OPTIONAL

¼ teaspoon dried herbs or spices of your choice

This bouncy-textured coconut-based wrap is made with mostly eggs. It cooks on the stovetop, almost like an omelet.

1. Add the coconut flour, eggs, milk, and salt and pepper to the bowl of a stand mixer. Combine the ingredients on low speed until the batter is smooth, about 3 minutes.

2. Turn off the mixer and allow the batter to sit for 5 minutes to help the coconut flour absorb moisture. The batter should be runny. If it's a little too thick, add an extra tablespoon of milk.

3. Place the oil in a skillet (with a lid) over medium-high heat. Pour ¼ cup of the batter into the skillet and immediately tilt it in different directions to create an 8-inch circle.

4. Place the lid on the skillet and cook the mixture for 1 or 2 minutes, or until the edges are golden, slightly turned inward, and bubbles form in the middle.

5. Flip the wrap, cover the skillet again, and cook the wrap for 1 or 2 minutes, or until it is browned.

6. Repeat the process until all the batter is used up.

Macros per 1-wrap serving (made with whole dairy milk and optional ingredients): 121 calories, 4.1 g net carbs, 9.9 g total carbs, 5.8 g fiber, 2.2 g sugars, 6.3 g total fat, 6.6 g protein

Iceberg Wrappers

Yield varies

Iceberg lettuce

Iceberg lettuce is the butt of many culinary jokes. True, it's mostly water and some fiber, but wow, does it make an excellent keto sandwich wrapper. As hardy as iceberg is, however, it can be a bit fiddly in the wrap department. Here is a quick rundown on how to use the leaves:

1. Choose a head that is large and unblemished; its leaves will be the best.

2. Without cutting into the lettuce leaves, remove the core at the base of the head.

3. If there are any withered or torn leaves on the outside of the head, gently remove them.

4. Fill a large mixing bowl or pot with cold water. Gently submerge the head of lettuce, holding it under the water if it floats up. Your goal is to get water between the all the leaves in the head. This helps separate them in a way that keeps the leaves whole and tear free. (You can also do this by simply turning your faucet on and allowing water to run into and through the head of lettuce.)

5. While the lettuce is under water, gently remove the leaves, stacking them in a colander or laying them flat on a clean dishtowel.

continued on next page

Iceberg Wrappers, continued

6. To use as a wrap, spoon filling in the lower third of the leaf, fold in the vertical sides of the leaf, and then roll it up the same way you'd roll a burrito.

7. Unused leaves can be stacked between dry paper towels and stored in the refrigerator for up to 2 days for future use in any salad or sandwich recipe.

Macros per serving (made with 1 large lettuce leaf): 2 calories, 0.1 g net carbs, 0.2 g total carbs, 0.1 g fiber, 0.1 g sugars, 0 g total fat, 0.1 g protein

Keto Deli Wrap

Makes 1 serving

1 slice deli turkey

1 slice deli ham

1 slice deli cheese

OPTIONAL

Dill pickle spear

Mustard

This easy deli wrap uses only deli slices (meat and cheese). Feel free to use different kinds of deli meat and cheese—whatever combos you use will be delicious!

1. Place the slice of deli turkey on a flat surface, and then place the ham and the cheese directly on top of it.

2. If you're using a pickle spear, place it on the bottom edge of the cheese. Squirt or spread a little mustard onto the pickle.

3. At the end, where the pickle is, roll the turkey and ham into a tube. It's ready to eat.

Macros per serving (made without optional ingredients): 150 calories, 3.6 g net carbs, 4.2 g total carbs, 0.6 g fiber, 1 g sugars, 8 g total fat, 11.6 g protein

Stacked Un-Sandwich

Makes 1 serving

1 cup Sandwich Salad (see page 31), Slow Cooker Pulled Pork (see page 37), Make-Ahead Chicken (see page 34), or cooked meat of choice, diced

1 cup shredded romaine lettuce or green cabbage

½ cup Stay-Fresh Keto Guacamole (see page 28)

½ cup cubed or shredded cheese

OPTIONAL

1 Perfect Hard-Boiled Egg (see page 20), chopped

1 or 2 slices Make-Ahead Bacon (see page 16), chopped

This recipe reminds me of a trifle, the sweet layered pudding served in a glass bowl, except this recipe uses savory sandwich ingredients instead of sweet dessert components. It's the perfect way to get the taste of a sandwich without wraps, buns, or bread.

1. Layer ½ cup of the sandwich salad or meat, ½ cup of the romaine lettuce, ¼ cup guacamole, ¼ cup cheese, and any of the optional ingredients you'd like to use in a Mason jar or other container.

2. Finish with a second layer of the remaining sandwich salad or meat, romaine lettuce, guacamole, and cheese.

Macros per serving: Calorie, fat, protein, and carb counts will vary with what you use in your stacked sandwich.

Low-Carb Turkey and Sweet Potato Slider

Makes 4 servings

1 tablespoon avocado oil, coconut oil, extra-virgin olive oil, or another oil

1 to 2 large sweet potatoes (enough for 8 large slices)

8 slices turkey deli meat (or use leftover turkey meat)

4 slices of deli Havarti cheese

OPTIONAL

Salt and pepper, to taste

Dash of cayenne or chile powder

Mayonnaise

Mustard

TIP When buying sweet potatoes for this recipe, search for ones that have a round shape and wide circumference, as they will make better "buns."

Because root veggies have a high carb content, they aren't eaten on the keto diet very often. However, using two slices of sweet potato in place of traditional slider rolls will save you carbs and supply your daily requirement for vitamin A.

1. Preheat the oven to 400°F.

2. In a large bowl, whisk together the oil and optional salt, pepper, and spice.

3. Add the sweet potato slices to the bowl and turn them in the oil mixture, making sure that the slices are evenly coated.

4. Arrange the sweet potato slices on a baking sheet and bake them in the oven for 12 minutes. Use an offset spatula to turn over the slices.

5. Bake the slices for another 12 minutes, or until they're just fork tender.

6. Allow the sweet potato slices to cool before using them. (Store any extras in a covered container in the refrigerator for up to 2 days.)

7. If desired, spread the inside of 2 sweet potato slices with mayonnaise and/or mustard, and layer 2 slices of turkey and 1 slice of cheese between the slices. Repeat with the remaining slices.

Macros per serving (made with avocado oil and without optional ingredients): 292 calories, 6 g net carbs, 12.9 g total carbs, 5.9 g fiber, 8 g sugars, 13.6 g total fat, 25.1 g protein

KETO BUNS

A lot of people like to make their sandwiches with rolls or buns—me included! I am happy to report that there are many keto-friendly alternatives to sandwich buns. Here are my go-to recipes.

Grilled Zucchini Buns

Makes 2 servings

1 tablespoon extra-virgin olive oil, avocado oil, coconut oil, or ghee

¼ teaspoon salt

¼ teaspoon pepper

¼ teaspoon of your favorite dried herb or spice

4½-inch-thick slices of a large zucchini

This easy veggie bun recipe uses an indoor grill pan or an outdoor grill.

1. In a large bowl, whisk together the oil, salt, pepper, and any chosen herb or spice.

2. Add the zucchini slices to the bowl and turn them in the mixture until they're well coated.

3. Heat a grill pan over medium-high heat. Place the zucchini slices on the grill and cook them for 2 minutes on each side, or until grill marks are visible and the zucchini is barely fork tender.

4. Layer the zucchini slices with your favorite sandwich fillings.

5. Store unused zucchini in a covered container in the refrigerator for up to 2 days.

Macros per serving (made with extra-virgin olive oil): 70 calories, 1.4 g net carbs, 2.1 g total carbs, 0.7 g fiber, 1 g sugars, 7.1 g total fat, 0.8 g protein

Eggplant Buns

Makes 2+ servings

1 small to medium eggplant

3 tablespoons extra-virgin olive oil, avocado oil, or coconut oil

½ teaspoon salt

½ teaspoon pepper

OPTIONAL

¼ teaspoon of your favorite dried herb or spice

TIP If you have extra eggplant buns, you can chop them and add to any keto recipe.

Eggplant is a fun, economical, easy-to-use vegetable for bun-making. This recipe will most likely make more than 2 servings, depending upon how large the eggplant is.

1. Preheat the oven to 425°F. Line a baking sheet with foil and set it aside.

2. Slice the eggplant evenly into ¾-inch-thick rounds. Arrange the rounds in a single layer on the prepared pan.

3. Drizzle half the oil evenly over the eggplant, then flip each eggplant slice and drizzle the remaining oil on the other side. Season the eggplant with the salt and pepper and optional herbs or spices.

4. Bake the eggplant slices for 18 to 20 minutes, or until each slice is browned on the outside and just fork tender. (You don't want the eggplant to get too soft or mushy.)

5. Remove the eggplant slices from the oven and allow them to cool. Extras can be stored in a covered container in the refrigerator for up to 2 days.

Macros per serving (made with extra-virgin olive oil): 205 calories, 2.4 g net carbs, 5.9 g total carbs, 3.5 g fiber, 3 g sugars, 21.2 g total fat, 1 g protein

Portobello Buns

Makes 1 serving

2 portobello mushroom caps, gills removed

½ tablespoon extra-virgin olive oil, avocado oil, coconut oil, or ghee

¼ teaspoon garlic powder

1 teaspoon dried oregano

Salt and pepper, to taste

TIP is important to clean portobello caps by scraping out the gills (the frills on the underside of the mushroom cap that can turn slimy when cooked and that often hide grit). Use the side of a small spoon to scrape off the gills and then discard them.

Mushroom buns are very popular in the keto community. If you've never made them, you're in for a treat: The buns are easy to make—they come together quickly with few ingredients—and, most importantly, they are outrageously good.

1. In a large bowl, whisk together the oil, garlic, oregano, and salt and pepper.

2. Add the mushroom caps to the bowl and rub the seasoned oil into the caps.

3. Preheat a frying pan over high heat. (You could also use a ridged grill pan.) Add the mushroom caps to the pan and cook for 4 to 5 minutes on each side, or until they're fork tender.

4. Use the mushrooms immediately or allow them to cool before using them as buns for your favorite fillings.

5. Store unused mushroom caps in a covered container in the refrigerator for up to 2 days.

Macros per serving made with extra virgin olive oil: 100 calories, 4 g net carbs, 6 g total carbs, 2 g fiber, 0 g sugars, 7 g total fat, 6 g protein

Smoked Trout Hoagie

Makes 1 serving

½ cup chopped smoked
   trout

2 tablespoons mayonnaise

1 teaspoon Dijon mustard

1 medium (or large)
   cucumber, peeled, halved
   lengthwise, and seeded

OPTIONAL

½ to 1 teaspoon minced
   fresh dill

Salt and pepper, to taste

TIP To seed a cucumber with
ease, halve the cucumber, then
use a spoon to scoop out the
"seedy marrow" that runs down
the center of the vegetable.

I love the idea of using a hollowed-out cucumber as a hoagie roll. It is so clever! The combination of smoked trout and cucumber is delicious, but feel free to use an equal amount of another protein, such as smoked whitefish, smoked salmon, Perfect Hard-Boiled Egg (see page 20), or leftover chicken as filling for this unique "roll."

1. In a large bowl, combine the trout, mayonnaise, mustard, and optional ingredients, then gently mix them until they're well combined. Adjust the seasoning to taste.

2. Fill the center depression in each cucumber half with half the fish mixture. Put the cucumber halves together, as if they were halves of a hoagie roll. Wrap them in parchment paper (or other food wrap) and store them in the fridge (up to 12 hours) until you're ready to eat.

Macros per serving (made with optional ingredients): 440 calories, 5 g net carbs, 8 g total carbs, 3 g fiber, 3 g sugars, 22 g total fat, 45 g protein

Keto Noodle Bowl

Makes 1 serving

1 tablespoon Keto Vinaigrette (see page 26)

1 tablespoon mayonnaise

1 medium zucchini, spiralized (or half a 10-ounce package of premade spiralized zucchini noodles)

¼ cup feta cheese, chopped

1 Perfect Hard-Boiled Egg (see page 20), chopped

OPTIONAL

Salt and pepper, to taste

2 tablespoons chopped black olives

¼ cup chopped chicken, shrimp, lamb, or another protein

If you haven't yet ventured into the world of spiralized veggies, now's the time. They are just the thing to help keto eaters enjoy "pasta" while still staying true to their low-carb diet. This flavorful bowl is a ketogenic spin on the ever-popular pasta salad.

1. Whisk together the vinaigrette and mayonnaise in a sealable food container.

2. Add the spiralized zucchini to the container and toss it in the vinaigrette mixture to coat.

3. Add the feta, egg, and any optional ingredients to the container. Do not toss them.

4. Eat the veggies immediately or store them in a sealed container in the fridge for up to 2 days.

Macros per serving (made without optional ingredients): 371 calories, 5.5 g net carbs, 10 g total carbs, 4.5 g fiber, 4 g sugars, 31.2 g total fat, 13.4 g protein

Burrito Bowl

Makes 1 serving

¾ cup chopped chicken thigh or breast meat (see Make-Ahead Chicken, page 34) or Seasoned Ground Beef (see page 40)

2 teaspoons chile powder

3 or 4 pickled jalapeño slices, minced

2 cups cauliflower rice, cooked per package instructions

½ tablespoon Keto Vinaigrette (see page 26)

OPTIONAL

Salt and pepper, to taste

Toppings, including chopped fresh cilantro, sliced Hass avocado, Stay-Fresh Keto Guacamole (see page 28), shredded cheese, etc.

Mexican-themed bowls are my absolute favorite, which is why I love this one. Feel free to personalize it by switching in other veggies and seasonings—whatever you like.

1. In a small bowl, stir together the chopped chicken or loose meat, 1 teaspoon of the chile powder, and the minced jalapenos. Set aside.

2. Spoon the prepared cauliflower rice onto the bottom of a sealable food container. Stir in the vinaigrette and the remaining 1 teaspoon chile powder.

3. Add the chicken mixture directly on top of the cauliflower rice. Do not stir.

4. Add toppings of your choice.

5. Enjoy the bowl immediately or seal and place it in the fridge for up to 3 days.

Macros per serving (made with chicken breast and without optional ingredients): 230 calories, 3 g net carbs, 5 g total carbs, 2 g fiber, 2 g sugars, 9 g total fat, 34 g protein

Keto Bowl
BLUEPRINT

Makes 1 serving

2 tablespoons (or more or less) Keto Vinaigrette (see page 26) or your favorite salad dressing

1 Hass avocado, chopped

2 cups cooked (or canned) fish, seafood, poultry, or red meat of your choice

2 cups chopped cooked or raw vegetables, including riced cauliflower or broccoli stems

Bowls began showing up on fast food and takeout menus shortly after the paleo and gluten-free eating movements started picking up steam. The premise was smart enough: get rid of not-so-healthful, carb-heavy ingredients such as bread, tortillas, and pasta and keep the healthy protein and plants. Brilliant, right?

But, as a keto eater, you also know that those trendy grain and bean bowls contain way too many carbs for your eating plan. Fortunately, there is an easy way to enjoy a lunch bowl in a keto-approved way: Make your own. In fact, you can put together a bowl with just about anything in your kitchen—even if you have only small amounts of this and that. Plus, bowls are super portable: Just layer the ingredients in a Mason jar or "grab-and-go" container, toss it in your bag, and you have an easy lunch (or breakfast or dinner, for that matter). But if you need a blueprint, this one comes in handy.

1 tablespoon (or more) favorite herb or mix of herbs

1 garlic clove, minced

¼ cup minced red onions, scallions, or shallots

Salt and pepper, to taste

½ cup shredded or cubed cheese

1 Perfect Hard-Boiled Egg (see page 20), chopped

1 or 2 slices Make-Ahead Bacon (see page 16), chopped

½ cup or more shredded unsweetened coconut

1. Add the vinaigrette, optional herbs, garlic, onions, salt, and pepper to a Mason jar or other container and shake until everything is well combined.

2. Add the avocado to the dressing and toss it gently, just until the avocado is evenly coated. Adjust salt and pepper to taste.

3. Add seafood, poultry, or meat and optional cheese, egg, bacon, and coconut on top of the dressing. Do not stir! Allow the dressing and avocado to sit at the bottom of the container until you are ready to eat.

4. Place the lid on the container and store it in the refrigerator.

5. Before eating, gently shake the container to distribute the dressing, then pour over the bowl of ingredients.

Macros per serving: Calorie, fat, protein, and carb counts will vary with what you decide to use to make your bowl.

7 | FAT BOMBS AND FATTY SNACKS

SNACKING GETS A BAD RAP, AND WITH GOOD REASON: FREQUENT

consumption of junky, high-carb processed food has made

many people obese. But in the keto world, snacking can be

strategic. And smart. As long as you are noshing on the right

thing. Eating a small fatty snack instead of a full meal—or

between meals—can help you reach and maintain ketosis,

which is an important goal for keto eaters.

Crispy Cheese Squares

Makes 36 to 44 crackers

10 to 12 ounces thinly sliced cheese of your choice (cheddar, provolone, Swiss, etc.)

I don't usually buy sliced cheese, as I try to purchase food in its "whole state" as often as possible. However, these crispy squares really work best with a pouch of sliced deli cheese. (And by this, I mean 100 percent cheese—not American processed cheese slices in individual wrappers.) They're insanely easy to make!

1. Preheat the oven to 250°F.

2. Line a baking sheet with foil or parchment paper.

3. Gently remove one cheese slice from the package and lay it flat on a cutting board. Cut the slice into four equal squares. Gently lift and place the squares on the prepared baking sheet, making sure none of them is touching.

4. Bake the squares for 25 to 30 minutes, or until they're golden and almost firm.

5. Remove the baking sheet from the oven and allow the cheese squares to cool on the baking sheet for 15 minutes.

6. Store the cheese squares in a single layer in a covered container for up to 3 days.

Macros per 12-cracker serving (made with cheddar cheese): 135 calories, 1 g net carbs, 1 g total carbs, 0 g fiber, 0 g sugars, 11 g fat, 8 g protein

Salami Chips

Makes 5 to 6 servings

1 (5- or 6-ounce) package of presliced salami or other cured, hard sausage

This fantastic keto snack may be even easier to make than the Crispy Cheese Squares at left! The recipe calls for a package of presliced salami (any variety is fine; I like Italian dry-style salami). You can also use presliced pepperoni or another cured hard sausage; you could even slice your own if you have a chub of cured sausage.

1. Preheat the oven to 325°F.

2. Line a large plate or platter with paper towels. Set it aside.

3. Place slices of salami in a single layer on a baking sheet, allowing space between slices.

4. Bake the salami for 10 to 15 minutes, or until the edges began to crisp.

5. Remove the baking sheet from the oven. Using a thin, metal spatula, gently transfer the salami chips from the baking sheet to the paper-towel lined platter and allow the chips to cool for about 10 minutes. They will continue to firm up as they cool.

5. Store any uneaten the salami in a covered container in the refrigerator for up to 5 days.

Macros per 1-ounce serving (about 8 slices Italian dry-style salami): 100 calories, 2 g net carbs, 2 g total carbs, 0 g fiber, 1 g sugars, 7 g fat, 7 g protein

Keto Deli Roll-Up

Makes 1 serving

1 slice deli poultry, such as smoked turkey, roast turkey, or chicken

1 slice deli pork-based or beef-based meat, such as ham, prosciutto, roast beef, pastrami, etc.

1 large leaf iceberg lettuce

1 slice deli cheese, such as American, cheddar, Swiss, provolone, etc.

OPTIONAL

1 teaspoon mustard

1 teaspoon mayonnaise

In this recipe, cheese and meat form a wrap to encase sandwich ingredients. You can use whatever you have in the fridge for this easy, creative, and fun snack.

1. Place a piece of deli poultry on a flat surface. Add a slice of pork- or beef-based deli meat on top.

2. Next, stack the lettuce and cheese.

3. If you are using mustard and mayonnaise as optional ingredients, spread them evenly on top of the cheese.

4. Starting from the outer, longer edge of the stack, roll the ingredients into a tube. If you need something to secure the wrap, pierce the rolled ingredients with a toothpick.

5. Eat the roll-up immediately or wrap it tightly in plastic wrap and store it in the fridge for up to 12 hours.

Macros per serving (using turkey breast, ham, and provolone cheese):
273 calories, 2.6 g net carbs, 3.3 g total carbs, 0.7 g fiber, 1.1 g sugars, 21.8 g fat, 15.7 g protein

B.A.E. Bites

Makes 6 servings

1 Perfect Hard-boiled Egg (see page 20)

¼ Hass avocado mashed with 1 teaspoon lime juice (to prevent browning)

6 tablespoons reserved bacon grease, ghee, melted butter, or a combination of fats

1 tablespoon mayonnaise

6 slices Make-Ahead Bacon (see page 16), finely chopped

OPTIONAL

½ tablespoon chopped fresh cilantro

Salt and pepper, to taste

B is for bacon, savory and delicious. A is for avocado, fatty and rich. And E is for egg, the keto diet's poster child! This recipe doubles well.

1. In the bowl of a food processor, combine the hard-boiled egg, avocado, bacon grease (or whatever fat you are using), mayonnaise, and optional ingredients, if you are using them. Pulse the mixture until it turns into a smooth paste.

2. Transfer the mixture to a large bowl, cover it, and place it in the refrigerator for 45 minutes or longer until the mixture is completely chilled.

3. Crumble the bacon into small bits in a small bowl. Set it aside.

4. Line a baking sheet with waxed paper or aluminum foil.

5. Remove the mixture from the fridge and, using a spoon and your hands or a small scoop, fashion 6 balls, dropping each one into the bowl of chopped bacon and rolling it around until it is fully coated.

6. Gently place the coated ball on the prepared baking sheet.

7. Repeat the process until all 6 coated balls are placed on the baking sheet.

8. Refrigerate the bites for 10 minutes or so, until they become firm. Enjoy them immediately or place them in a single layer in a covered food storage container and keep them in the fridge. As long as they're covered, they'll be good for a couple days.

Macros per 1-piece serving (made with optional ingredients): 185 calories, 1 g net carbs, 1 g total carbs, 0.5 g fiber, 0.5 g sugars, 19 g fat, 5 g protein

3-Ingredient Crackers

Makes 6 servings (about 30 crackers)

1 large egg

2 cups almond flour (or almond meal), or another nut flour, such as pecan, peanut, walnut, or hazelnut

½ teaspoon salt

OPTIONAL

⅛ to ¼ teaspoon cayenne, black pepper, garlic salt, or another favorite spice; or sesame seeds or poppy seeds

If you are a keto eater who loves crispy snacks, you know how expensive store-bought low-carb crackers can be. This delicious (and easy) recipe can help give your wallet a break. The directions appear a bit more involved than many of the recipes in this chapter, but everything goes together easily. I promise!

1. Preheat the oven to 350°F.

2. In a large bowl, add the egg and beat it with a whisk.

3. Gently stir the flour, salt, and as many optional ingredients as you like. Stir until the mixture is well blended.

4. Place 1 long sheet (approximately 12 inches) of waxed or parchment paper on a countertop or table. Transfer the dough from the bowl onto the waxed paper and press the dough into a disk with your hands.

5. Place another long sheet of waxed or parchment paper on top of the disk of dough. Using a rolling pin, roll the dough into a large rectangle. The dough should be about 1/16 to ⅛ inch thick.

6. Gently lift the paper and dough and place in the refrigerator. Let the dough chill for at least 15 minutes. This will make it easier to handle in the next steps.

7. Remove the chilled dough from the fridge and peel away the top layer of paper.

8. Using a paring knife or a pizza cutter, cut the dough into 1½ x 2½-inch rectangular crackers.

9. Prick each cracker 2 or 3 times with the tines of a fork.

10. Line an ungreased baking sheet with a piece of foil.

11. Using an offset spatula, gently transfer the crackers to the baking sheet.

12. Bake the crackers for 10 to 12 minutes, or until they're golden and slightly firm to the touch (they'll firm up further once they're removed from the oven).

13. Enjoy the crackers immediately or store them in an airtight container for up to 10 days.

Macros per serving (5 crackers, using almond flour and no optional spice): 224 calories, 4 g net carbs, 8 g total carbs, 4 g fiber, 1 g sugars, 19.5 g fat, 9.5 g protein

Keto Queso Dip

Makes about 2½ cups

1 cup canned coconut
cream

1½ cups cheddar cheese
(sharp or mild), finely
shredded or grated

OPTIONAL

Pinch of chipotle or chile
powder or 1 tablespoon
minced jalapeño or
poblano chilies

**Who doesn't love cheese dip? This one is quick, easy, and keto
compliant. Use whatever you like as a dipper, from spears
of roasted asparagus to chunks of chicken and any of the
3-Ingredient Crackers (see page 104). Keto Queso Dip is so
versatile you can also use it as a sandwich spread or a sauce
for poultry or veggies, if you warm it up and thin it with a few
teaspoons of water.**

1. Place the coconut cream in a small saucepan over medium
heat for about 3 minutes, until it is just warm.

2. Slowly stir in the cheese, 1 tablespoon at a time, until the
cheese is fully incorporated.

3. Add optional spice and mix it in thoroughly.

4. Using a spatula, scrape the cheese dip into a serving bowl
and enjoy it immediately.

Macros per serving (2 tablespoons, made with a pinch of chipotle powder):
59 calories, 0.5 g net carbs, 0.8 g total carbs, 0.3 g fiber, 0.4 g sugars, 5.5 g fat,
2.2 g protein

Braunschweiger Balls

Makes 12 servings

8 ounces liverwurst, at room temperature

6 ounces cream cheese, softened

¼ cup chopped pecans

1 to 2 teaspoons mustard

8 slices crispy Make-Ahead Bacon (see page 16), finely chopped

OPTIONAL

Salt and pepper, to taste

Made with Braunschweiger (aka liverwurst), these fat bombs are high in iron and protein, with a delicious flavor and plenty of fat (thanks to you, dear bacon). You'll love this no-cook recipe.

1. Place the liverwurst, cream cheese, pecans, mustard, and salt and pepper (if you're using them), in a food processor and pulse until the mixture is just combined.

2. Using a small cookie scoop or a large spoon, scoop out 12 portions of the mixture and roll it into balls.

3. Place the balls on a plate or baking sheet and chill in the refrigerator for at least 30 minutes.

4. After 30 minutes or more, remove the balls from the fridge and roll each of them in a bowl containing the bacon bits. Eat them immediately or store the balls in a covered container in the fridge for up to 5 days. Serve them cold or at room temperature.

Macros per 1-ball serving (made with optional ingredients): 194 calories, 1.3 g net carbs, 1.6 g total carbs, 0.3 g fiber, 0.8 g sugars, 16.9 g fat, 9 g protein

Meaty Jalapeño Poppers

Makes 8 servings

6 ounces ground beef, bison, chorizo, or another ground meat

1 garlic clove, minced

8 medium jalapeños, halved, seeds removed

2 ounces cream cheese, softened

OPTIONAL

1 teaspoon ground cumin

1 teaspoon dried oregano

Salt and black pepper, to taste

This keto-friendly riff on the beloved appetizer uses fresh jalapeño peppers and cream cheese. If you have leftover meatloaf, meatballs, or bacon, you can crumble it up and substitute it for the ground meat, garlic, and spices in the ingredient list and skip step 2. Just add the leftover meat and begin with step 3.

1. Preheat the oven to 350°F and lightly grease a baking sheet with a bit of ghee, butter, coconut oil, avocado oil, olive oil, lard, or bacon fat.

2. Place a large sauté pan over medium heat. Add the meat, garlic, and optional cumin and oregano to the pan and cook the meat until it is well browned. Season the meat with optional salt and pepper. Set the pan aside.

3. Smear each of the 16 jalapeño halves with cream cheese, leaving room for the meat mixture. Once the meat mixture has cooled, spoon about 1 teaspoon into each jalapeño half.

4. Place the poppers on the prepared baking sheet and bake for 30 minutes.

5. Eat the poppers immediately or store them in the refrigerator for up to 5 days.

Macros per 2-popper serving (made with ground beef and optional ingredients): 80 calories, 0.8 g net carbs, 1.2 g total carbs, 0.4 g fiber, 0.5 g sugars, 5.6 g fat, 6 g protein

Creamy Salmon Bombs

Makes about 8 servings

½ cup cream cheese, softened

⅓ cup butter, softened

8 ounces smoked salmon

1 tablespoon fresh lemon juice

OPTIONAL

1 to 2 tablespoons freshly chopped dill (or 1 teaspoon dried), plus more for garnish

Salt and pepper, to taste

This recipe is ideal for brunch or a dinner appetizer and can also be used as a dip or spread. Feel free to substitute the salmon with another smoked fish (whitefish is lovely).

1. Line a tray with parchment paper. Set it aside.

2. Place all the ingredients (including optional ingredients, if you are using them) in the bowl of a food processor. Pulse the mixture until smooth.

3. Using a cookie scoop or a large spoon, create small fat bombs using about 2½ tablespoons of the mixture per portion. Garnish with more dill and place in the refrigerator for 1 or 2 hours, or until firm.

4. Eat as is or on top of crunchy lettuce leaves or enjoy as a spread on cucumber slices or with spears of endive or romaine. Store in the refrigerator for up to 5 days.

Macros per 2½-tablespoon serving (made with optional ingredients):
62 calories, 0.9 g net carbs, 0.9 g total carbs, 0 g fiber, 0.8 g sugars, 14.9 g fat, 6.4 g protein

Snow Balls

Makes 12 servings

¼ cup cocoa butter

¼ cup coconut oil

¼ cup finely shredded unsweetened coconut

5 to 10 drops liquid stevia

½ teaspoon pure vanilla extract

Are you a white chocolate fan? If so, you will find these creamy fat bombs thoroughly addictive. Personalize this recipe with spices, extracts, or add-ins such as dried coconut, chocolate chips, or nuts.

1. Place the cocoa butter and coconut oil in a double boiler set over low heat.

2. When the cocoa butter and coconut oil have melted, remove the pan from the heat and stir in the shredded coconut, stevia, and vanilla.

3. Pour the mixture into 12 small molds or mini muffin cups.

4. Chill the mixture in the refrigerator until it has hardened, about an hour.

5. Remove the snow balls from the molds. Eat them immediately or store them in a covered container in the refrigerator for up to 10 days.

Macros per 1-ball serving: 183 calories, 2.5 g net carbs, 5 g total carbs, 2.5 g fiber, 1.3 g sugars, 19.3 g fat, 1.3 g protein

Nut Butter Fudge

Makes 12 servings

1 cup unsweetened peanut butter, almond butter, or another nut or seed butter of your choice

1 cup coconut oil

¼ cup unsweetened coconut milk, coconut cream, or dairy cream

OPTIONAL

Pinch of salt, only if needed

Dash of pure vanilla extract or a sprinkle of cinnamon or nutmeg

1 to 2 teaspoons liquid stevia

Unsweetened shredded coconut

You want easy? Here it is. This quick-to-make treat consists of nut butter, coconut oil, and coconut milk. That's it. Of course, you can change things up by adding your favorite spices or extracts.

1. Slightly melt or soften the peanut butter and coconut oil together in a small saucepan set over low heat or in a microwave-safe bowl in the microwave.

2. Add the warm mixture, along with all the remaining ingredients, except the shredded coconut, to the bowl of a food processor or stand mixer and process until the ingredients are well combined and smooth.

3. Line a mini muffin pan with paper liners. Pour the mixture into the liners, sprinkling a pinch of shredded coconut over each.

4. Refrigerate the tray for about 2 hours, until the fudge has set. Eat it immediately or store the fudge in an airtight container in the refrigerator for up to 10 days.

Macros per 1-piece serving (made with peanut butter, coconut milk, and optional flavorings, but no coconut): 294 calories, 3.1 g net carbs, 4.5 g total carbs, 1.4 g fiber, 2.2 g sugars, 30.2 g fat, 5.5 g protein

Keto Cheesecake Pops

Makes 4 servings

1 (8-ounce) block of cream cheese (do not used "whipped cream cheese")

¼ teaspoon stevia extract (or more, to taste)

2 tablespoons heavy cream

1 teaspoon lemon or lime juice

If you love cheesecake, you'll adore these easy-to-make freezer bombs—they're a delicious alternative to commercially made ice cream and frozen confections (which happen to be loaded with carbs). You'll need an ice pop mold to make these perfectly creamy lime-flavored cheesecakes.

1. Place all the ingredients in a blender and puree until smooth.

2. Taste. Adjust the stevia, if desired.

3. Pour the mixture into ice pop molds and freeze for 4 hours or until completely frozen.

Macro counts per serving (made with ¼ teaspoon stevia extract and lemon juice): 224 calories, 1.7 g net carbs, 1.7 g total carbs, 0 g fiber, 0.12 g sugars, 22.5 g fat, 4.4 g protein

DIY Sweet Bomb
BLUEPRINT

Yield varies

- 1 cup fat, or a mixture of 2 or 3 fats (including avocado, avocado oil, butter, cocoa butter, coconut butter, coconut cream, coconut oil, cream cheese, ghee, heavy cream, nut butter, or sour cream)

- 1 tablespoon or more flavoring (dark chocolate, 1 teaspoon of pure vanilla extract, spices, a few drops of peppermint extract, etc.)

- 2 tablespoons to ¼ cup texture- and bulk-giving ingredients, such as shredded coconut, chia, cacao nibs, nuts, or seeds

If you have a blueprint, you can easily customize this basic recipe to make endless combinations of yummy, healthy, fabulous fat bombs, using whatever you have on hand. Try it!

1. Place all the ingredients in a large bowl and whisk them together until they are thoroughly combined. If it makes sense to use a food processor or blender, do so, pulsing the ingredients together until they are well combined.

2. Pour the mixture into small cups or molds. (I like to use mini muffin cups.)

3. Freeze or refrigerate sweet bombs until they're solid. (Times will vary depending upon ingredients.)

4. Store the bombs in a cool place or refrigerate them in an airtight container for up to 10 days.

NOTE If you're using nuts or seeds, less is more. These ingredients are best used in small amounts because they tend to be high in carbohydrates.

Macros per serving: Will vary depending upon what ingredients are used.

8 | DINNER AND OTHER LARGE MEALS

SETTLING IN AT THE END OF THE DAY WITH A GOOD MEAL IS AN

important way in our culture to unwind and connect (either with ourselves, if dining alone, or with others). We like our end-of-day meal to be a bit special, but no one wants to spend a lot of time meal-making after a long day. The collection of recipes in this chapter varies from almost instant (and super easy) to a bit more involved (but so worth the work).

Cilantro Lime Shrimp Scampi, served with Zucchini Noodles

Makes 4 servings

2 tablespoons extra-virgin olive oil, butter, or coconut oil

1 pound jumbo shrimp (16 to 24 count), shelled and deveined

4 garlic cloves, chopped

¼ cup Chicken Bone Broth (recipe page 24)

Prepared base of choice, such as spiralized zucchini noodles or cauliflower rice

OPTIONAL (BUT HIGHLY RECOMMENDED)

2 tablespoons lime juice

Salt and pepper, to taste

2 tablespoons chopped fresh cilantro

I love this light, fresh-tasting "special occasion" recipe with spiralized zucchini noodles, but it's also good over spaghetti squash or riced cauliflower or broccoli.

1. Warm olive oil in a large sauté pan over medium-high heat. Add the shrimp, cook for 2 minutes, flip, add the garlic, and cook for 1 more minute, until the shrimp are pink and not opaque in the center. Place the shrimp in a bowl and set aside.

2. Add the broth and optional lime juice to the pan, deglaze it, and simmer for 2 minutes.

3. Return the shrimp to the pan with the salt and pepper and optional cilantro, tossing to combine. Remove from the heat and pour over prepared noodles or rice.

Macros per serving (made with extra-virgin olive oil, all optional ingredients, and spiralized zucchini): 520 calories, 3.6 g net carbs, 4.4 g total carbs, 0.8 g fiber, 0 g sugars, 12 g total fat, 90 g protein

Tuna Burgers

Makes 4 servings

2 (5-ounce) cans tuna (I like to use albacore tuna in oil, but any type will do), drained

2½ tablespoons almond flour

2 tablespoons mayonnaise

1 large egg, beaten

½ tablespoon extra-virgin olive oil or avocado oil, for the pan

OPTIONAL

Salt and pepper, to taste

1 tablespoon chopped fresh chives or dill (or 1 teaspoon dried)

1 scallion, chopped (or 1 tablespoon minced shallot or red onion)

1 tablespoon capers

These yummy patties can be enjoyed with any of the "keto buns" on page 89, or nestled on a mound of Cauliflower Mash (see page 126), spiralized veggie noodles, or salad. The burgers are made with canned tuna, making this the perfect "cupboard recipe."

1. In a bowl, gently combine all the ingredients (including optional ingredients), except the oil. Mix until all the ingredients are thoroughly combined.

2. Form the mixture into 4 patties, about ¾ inch thick (if they are too thick, they won't cook through the middle).

3. Pour the oil in a large skillet over medium-high heat and place the patties in the pan.

4. Cook the patties on one side for about 4 minutes, or until they have set and are golden.

5. Flip the patties and cook them on the other side for about 4 minutes, until golden.

6. Enjoy the tuna burgers immediately or allow them to cool and store them in the refrigerator in a closed container (keep the layers separate with some waxed paper) for up to 3 days.

Macros per serving (using extra-virgin olive oil and optional ingredients): 236 calories, 2.3 g net carbs, 2.8 g total carbs, 0.5 g fiber, 0.6 g sugars, 13 g total fat, 25 g protein

Salmon Steak over Shredded Zucchini

Makes 2 servings

2 (6- to 8-ounce) salmon steaks, about 1 inch thick

Salt and pepper, to taste

1½ tablespoons lemon juice

2 tablespoons butter, plus extra for sautéing the zucchini

1 medium to large zucchini, shredded (about two cups)

OPTIONAL

½ teaspoon garlic powder

Salmon is a keto favorite. This easy recipe comes together in minutes, for a complete keto meal. Try swapping crookneck squash for the zucchini, and feel free to add dried or fresh herbs to the salmon.

1. Pat the salmon steaks dry with paper towels. Season them all over with salt, pepper, and garlic powder, if you are using it, and then massage the lemon juice into each steak.

2. Place the butter in a large nonstick pan or skillet over medium-high heat. When the butter has melted, place the salmon steaks in the pan, pressing them lightly so the entire surface of the flesh comes into contact with the pan. Sear the steaks, undisturbed, for 2 to 3 minutes until the flesh is crispy and golden.

3. Turn the steaks and sear them on the other side for 2 to 3 minutes, until the flesh is crispy and golden.

4. If the fish isn't done, turn it back to the original side and cook for another 3 minutes or until a thermometer reads 145°F when inserted. You'll know the salmon is done when it begins to flake but still is slightly translucent in the middle.

5. When they're done, place each salmon steak on a dinner plate.

continued on next page

6. Add the shredded zucchini to the pan you used to cook the fish. If necessary, add 1 to 2 teaspoons of butter to the pan and allow it to melt before adding the zucchini.

7. Sauté the zucchini for 1 minute or less, just until the zucchini is barely tender. Season with salt, pepper, and garlic powder, if you like.

Macros per 8-ounce serving (made with optional ingredient): 750 calories, 2.6 g net carbs, 3.8 g total carbs, 1.2 g fiber, 2 g sugars, 30 g total fat, 50 g protein

FAUX RICE, PASTA, AND POTATOES

If you're like me, your favorite part of a saucy, comfort food meal is the rice, pasta, or potatoes that are served alongside. When you're on the keto diet, however, rice, pasta, and potatoes are no-nos. That doesn't mean you can't have comforting side dishes, though. Here are some popular keto-approved side dish substitutions.

Cauliflower Rice

Makes 4 servings

1 large head cauliflower, broken into 1-inch florets

3 tablespoons butter

2 garlic cloves, minced

Salt and pepper, to taste

OPTIONAL

1 or 2 teaspoons lemon juice, to prevent browning

2 tablespoons chopped fresh herbs, such as parsley or chives

This fun recipe can be customized with additional herbs or spices. Have fun with it.

1. Add the cauliflower to the bowl of a food processor and pulse until the cauliflower resembles rice. Depending on the size of your food processor, you will probably need to process the cauliflower in 2 to 3 batches. Place in a medium bowl and set aside.

2. Place the butter in a large skillet over medium-high heat. When the butter has melted, add the garlic and cauliflower and stir to combine. Season with salt and pepper.

3. Cook the cauliflower for 4 to 5 minutes, until the cauliflower just begins to soften.

4. Remove the pan from the heat, adjust salt and pepper, and stir in the lemon juice and fresh herbs, if you are using them.

Macros per serving (made without optional ingredients): 131 calories, 5.7 g net carbs, 11 g total carbs, 5.3 g fiber, 5 g sugars, 8.9 g total fat, 4.5 g protein

Broccoli Rice

Makes 2 servings

4 broccoli stalks, dried ends removed, cut into large chunks

1½ tablespoons butter

1 to 4 garlic cloves, minced

Salt and pepper, to taste

This recipe is a brilliant way to use up broccoli stalks. If you don't have a food processor, simply grate the broccoli on the coarsest side of a box grater.

1. Place the chunks of broccoli stalks in the bowl of a food processor and pulse until they are the size of rice grains. Do not overprocess.

2. Add the butter and garlic to a large sauté pan and set it over medium heat. Cook the garlic for a minute or two until it has softened.

3. Add the riced broccoli, salt, and pepper to the pan, and cook the broccoli for 8 to 10 minutes, until it is just tender.

Macros per serving: 125 calories, 5.4 g net carbs, 9 g total carbs, 3.6 g fiber, 0 g sugars, 9.1 g total fat, 0 g protein

Spiralized Veggie Pasta

Makes 1 or 2 servings

1 peeled and trimmed root, bulb, or zucchini (or other summer squash) or a 10 ounce container spiralized vegetables

1 tablespoon butter or another fat (bacon fat is nice)

Salt and pepper, to taste

This is a fun recipe if you have a spiralizer attachment for your stand mixer or food processor. You can also use a handheld spiralizer or—the easiest option—simply purchase a package of already spiralized veggies in the produce section of your local grocery store.

1. Using a spiralizer attachment on your food processor or stand mixer, or a mechanical spiralizer or handheld spiralizer, spiralize one vegetable per serving. (Large vegetables, such as rutabagas and eggplants, will make 2 or more servings.) If you are using prepared spiralized vegetables, skip this step.

2. Add the butter (or other fat) to a large sauté pan and set it over medium-high heat. When the butter melts, add the spiralized veggie (or veggies, for 2 portions) and sauté for 5 minutes, stirring gently to coat all the strands with butter.

3. Season with salt and pepper.

4. Use the spiralized veggie in your favorite recipe or store it in a covered container for up to 2 days in the fridge.

Macros per serving: Varies depending on which vegetable and fat you use for your veggie pasta

TIP Although vegetables should play an important role in your diet, they can be carb heavy. Stick to low-carb veggies, such as jicama, cucumber, turnip, rutabaga, kohlrabi, summer squash, zucchini, or eggplant for this dish.

Cauliflower Mash

Makes about 4 servings

1 large head cauliflower, cut into florets

3 tablespoons butter

2 tablespoons heavy cream

Salt and pepper, to taste

OPTIONAL

1 or 2 teaspoons lemon juice, to prevent browning

2 tablespoons chopped fresh herbs, such as parsley or chives

I first tasted mashed cauliflower in a macrobiotic cooking class back in the early 2000s. It was seasoned with miso paste and caramelized onions, and it was fantastic. This version—without miso—is just as fantastic!

1. Fill a large saucepot with salted water and place it over high heat. When the water comes to a boil, add the cauliflower. Boil until the cauliflower is fork tender.

2. While the cauliflower is still warm, transfer it to the bowl of a food processor. Add the butter, cream, salt and pepper, and lemon juice, if you're using it. Puree the mixture until it is smooth. (Alternatively, you can use an immersion blender to blend the butter and garlic into the cooked cauliflower.)

3. Adjust the seasoning and top with fresh herbs, if you like.

Macros per serving (made with optional ingredients): 137 calories, 5.2 g net carbs, 10.5 g total carbs, 5.3 g fiber, 0 g sugars, 9.5 g total fat, 4.4 g protein

Broccoli Mash

Makes 2 servings

2 cups broccoli florets and/
or peeled stalks

1½ tablespoons butter

1 small garlic clove

OPTIONAL

1 tablespoon chopped
fresh chives, parsley,
basil, or another herb

Salt and pepper, to taste

This bright green dish looks nothing like mashed potatoes, but it has that same smooth, creamy texture. Use peeled leftover broccoli stalks, or fresh or frozen broccoli florets.

1. Fill a large saucepot with salted water and place it over high heat. When the water comes to a boil, add the broccoli. Boil until the broccoli is fork tender.

2. While the broccoli is still warm, transfer it to the bowl of a food processor. Add the butter and garlic and pulse until the mixture is smooth. (Alternatively, you can use an immersion blender to blend the butter and garlic into the cooked broccoli.)

3. Add salt and pepper to taste. Sprinkle the mash with your choice of fresh herbs, if you like, and serve immediately. It will keep in the fridge for up to 2 days in a covered container.

Macros per serving (made without optional ingredients): 94 calories, 2.3 g net carbs, 3.5 g total carbs, 1.2 g fiber, 0.8 g sugars, 8.8 g total fat, 1.5 g protein

Leafy Green Lasagna

Makes 4 servings

1 tablespoon extra-virgin olive oil, plus extra for the baking dish

1 pound Italian sweet or hot sausage, casings removed

2 cups tomato puree

2 medium-size bunches of chard, ribs removed

2 cups grated mozzarella cheese

OPTIONAL

Salt and pepper, to taste

Garlic powder, to taste

1 tablespoon minced fresh basil or 1 teaspoon dried basil

This lasagna uses chard leaves instead of sheets of pasta. Try it!

1. Preheat the oven to 375°F.

2. Prepare a 9 × 12-inch baking dish by rubbing it with olive oil. Set it aside.

3. Place 1 tablespoon of extra-virgin olive oil in a large sauté pan over medium-high heat. Add the sausage and optional salt, pepper, garlic powder, and herbs, and cook until the sausage is browned, breaking it up with a spoon.

4. Add the tomato puree, more optional salt and pepper and herbs to taste, and let the mixture simmer for about 20 minutes, or until it is slightly reduced.

5. In the baking dish, layer half the chard, half the sauce, and 1 cup of the mozzarella.

6. Repeat with another layer of chard, sauce, and the remaining 1 cup mozzarella.

7. Cover the dish with foil and bake for about 15 minutes.

8. Remove the foil and bake another 20 minutes, or until the casserole is bubbling and the cheese is starting to brown.

9. Let the lasagna sit for about 10 minutes before serving.

Macros per serving (made with sweet Italian sausage and optional ingredients): 618 calories, 6 g net carbs, 11 g total carbs, 5 g fiber, 5 g sugars, 48 g total fat, 30 g protein

Keto Stuffed Peppers

Makes 2 servings

1½ cups small cauliflower florets

1 tablespoon extra-virgin olive oil

6 ounces Italian sweet or hot sausage, casing removed

½ cup grated provolone cheese

2 large red bell peppers

OPTIONAL

1 teaspoon dried basil, or a combination of dried basil and oregano, divided

Salt and pepper, to taste

When I was growing up, my mom would occasionally make stuffed peppers using green bell peppers, leftover meatloaf, and Minute Rice. I liked them . . . but I like these even more. Feel free to use a different color pepper, if you like.

1. Preheat the oven to 350°F.

2. Place the cauliflower in the bowl of a food processor and pulse until the cauliflower resembles rice.

3. Place the cauliflower rice, olive oil, half the optional herbs, and optional salt and pepper in a large sauté pan over medium heat. Cover the pan with a lid and let the cauliflower steam for about 6 minutes, until it is tender. Remove the pan from the heat and set it aside.

4. In another sauté pan, cook the sausage, the remaining half of the optional herbs, and optional salt and pepper, until the sausage is no longer pink. Set the pan aside.

5. Add the sausage, the fat from the pan, and the cauliflower rice to a large bowl with ¼ cup of the cheese. Stir the mixture to combine. Adjust seasonings if necessary. Set the bowl aside.

7. Prepare the peppers by gently cutting off the tops and removing the core and seeds. Cut the peppers in half lengthwise. You should have four pepper halves.

8. Place the peppers cut side up into a baking dish and spoon the sausage-cauliflower mixture into each pepper half. Top with a sprinkling of cheese.

9. Cover the dish with foil and bake the peppers for 25 minutes.

10. After 25 minutes, remove the foil and continue to bake the peppers for 10 minutes, or until the cheese is bubbly.

Macros per serving (made with optional ingredients): 514 calories, 5 g net carbs, 10 g total carbs, 5 g fiber, 4 g sugars, 42.5 g total fat, 23 g protein

Eggplant Roll-Ups

Makes 6 servings

1 large eggplant

Salt and pepper, to taste

1 cup cottage cheese or ricotta cheese

½ cup shredded mozzarella cheese

½ cup marinara sauce

OPTIONAL

Garlic powder, to taste

1 teaspoon Italian seasoning mix

¼ cup Parmesan cheese

I have always loved Italian-style rolled eggplant. This lower-carb version can be varied in infinite ways. Feel free to add sausage or switch up the cheeses or use more marinara sauce. It is all good (and delicious)!

1. Stand the eggplant, stem side up, and cut it lengthwise into ¼-inch slices, for a total of about 6 portions.

2. Rub both sides of each slice with salt and pepper.

3. Place the eggplant slices on a layer of paper towels and allow them to "sweat" for 15 to 20 minutes.

4. Preheat the oven to 350°F.

5. Pat the eggplant dry with fresh paper towels and transfer the slices to a rimmed baking sheet.

6. Bake the eggplant until it is barely tender, about 15 minutes. (Do not overcook it!)

7. While the eggplant slices are in the oven, place the cottage cheese, mozzarella, salt and pepper, and optional seasonings in a bowl and mix them together. Set the bowl aside

8. Remove the eggplant slices from the oven and allow them to rest for 5 minutes.

9. Raise the oven temperature to 400°F.

10. Spoon ¼ cup of the marinara sauce into the bottom of a 13 × 9-inch heatproof glass baking dish.

continued on next page

11. Spoon 2 tablespoons of the cottage cheese mixture onto an eggplant slice. Roll it up and place it, seam side down, on the marinara sauce in the baking dish. Repeat until all the eggplant slices have been rolled and placed in the baking dish.

12. Top the roll-ups with the remaining marinara sauce and optional Parmesan, and bake until the cheese is bubbly and the eggplant is tender, about 20 minutes.

Macros per serving (made with cottage cheese and all optional ingredients):
110 calories, 4 g net carbs, 7.4 g total carbs, 3.4 g fiber, 0 g sugars, 6 g total fat, 8.2 g protein

Shepherd's Keto Pie

Makes 6 servings

1½ pounds ground lamb (or a mix of ½ pound ground beef and 1 pound ground lamb)

2 garlic cloves, minced

1 tablespoon chopped fresh rosemary or 1 teaspoon dried rosemary

Salt and pepper, to taste

1 recipe Cauliflower Mash (see page 126) with lemon and herbs omitted, and ¼ cup shredded cheddar cheese stirred in at the end of the recipe

OPTIONAL

1 teaspoon onion powder

NOTE If you decide to use all ground beef, you'll have yourself a cottage pie.

Shepherd's pie is a popular pub casserole that features seasoned ground lamb (or ground lamb and beef) topped with a blanket of mashed potatoes. This yummy keto version replaces the carb-heavy potatoes with—you guessed it— Cauliflower Mash (see page 126).

1. Preheat the oven to 400°F.

2. Place the lamb, garlic, rosemary, salt and pepper, and optional onion powder in a large skillet over medium heat. Cook the meat for about 10 minutes, or until it has browned and is almost cooked through.

3. Transfer the meat to a 2-quart casserole dish.

4. Spread the Cauliflower Mash over the meat mixture in the casserole dish and bake, uncovered, for 20 minutes, or until the casserole is bubbling and golden.

5. Remove the casserole from the oven and let it sit for 10 minutes before serving.

Macros per serving (using lamb with optional ingredient): 400 calories, 4.5 g net carbs, 8.5 g total carbs, 4 g fiber, 0 g sugars, 28 g total fat, 29 g protein

Bacon Crust Pizza

Makes 4 servings

12 slices thick-cut bacon

¼ cup tomato puree, tomato sauce, or marinara sauce

¼ cup grated Parmesan cheese

1 cup shredded mozzarella cheese

NOTE Please read the recipe two or three times before you gather your ingredients to make this. There are a few items you'll want to have readily on hand.

This intriguing recipe is very different, and a bit fiddly, but it's so fun and delicious that I urge you to try it. Feel free to add toppings if you'd like.

A PIECE OF ADVICE A sharp pizza cutter or poultry/kitchen shears will do a better job of cutting than a regular knife.

1. Preheat the oven to 400°F.

2. Prepare a 13 × 9-inch baking sheet with foil or parchment paper.

3. Line 6 slices of bacon horizontally on the baking sheet.

4. Weave the remaining 6 bacon slices "into" the six horizontal pieces. This is where things get a bit fiddly, but once you get the hang of it, it is easy. Starting at the upper left corner, take a slice of bacon and lay it vertically over the horizontal bacon. Lift the bottom end of the vertical bacon and weave it underneath and above each of the horizontal pieces, as if you are weaving a basket.

5. Continue the process with the remaining 5 slices of bacon.

6. Weigh down the bacon with another 13 × 9-inch baking sheet or an ovenproof cooling rack.

7. Bake for 20 to 25 minutes, or until the bacon begins to crisp.

continued on next page

Bacon Crust Pizza, continued

8. Remove the baking sheet (with whatever item you've placed on top of the bacon to weigh it down) from the oven and gently tilt the baking sheet over a large heatproof bowl to pour off excess fat. You want to remove as much bacon grease as possible. (Save the grease in the fridge for up to 3 days to use in any savory recipe that calls for fat or oil.)

9. Spread tomato puree over the woven bacon. Then sprinkle it with Parmesan and mozzarella cheese and put it back in the oven.

10. Bake for another 5 to 10 minutes, until the cheese is melted.

11. Remove the pizza from the oven and allow it to cool for 10 minutes before cutting into quarters.

Macros per serving (made using tomato puree): 328 calories, 1.9 g net carbs, 2.2 g total carbs, 0.3 g fiber, 1.1 g sugars, 26 g total fat, 21 g protein

Slow Cooker Lamb Shanks served with Green Mash

Makes 4 servings

4 lamb shanks, trimmed

2 garlic cloves, minced

2 tablespoons tomato paste

4 teaspoons onion powder

Broccoli Mash recipe (see page 127), doubled

OPTIONAL

Salt and pepper, to taste

I lived in Australia as a young girl, which means we ate a lot of lamb. Lots of it! It wasn't until I attended culinary school in New York City, however, that I learned how to make lamb shanks. I was shocked at how easy it is to make such an elegant dish. This recipe makes it even easier, thanks to a slow cooker.

1. Place the lamb shanks in the slow cooker.

2. Sprinkle the minced garlic and optional salt and pepper over the lamb shanks.

3. Into 1 cup of water, whisk the tomato paste and onion powder. When fully combined, pour the mixture over the lamb shanks.

4. Cover and cook on low for 6 to 8 hours, until the meat falls off the bones.

Macros per serving (with optional ingredient, without Broccoli Mash):
437 calories, 1.6 g net carbs, 2 g total carbs, 0.4 g fiber, 1 g sugars, 15.9 g total fat, 67 g protein

Creamy Mushroom Pork Chops

Makes 6 servings

4 tablespoons butter

6 thick-cut pork chops, with or without the bone

Salt and pepper, to taste

2 cups sliced white, cremini, or other type of mushroom

1 cup heavy cream

OPTIONAL

4 garlic cloves, minced

1 teaspoon dried thyme

Rich, creamy, and comforting, these pork chops are delicious served with Broccoli Mash (see page 127) or any other green, low-carb veggie.

1. Melt the butter in a skillet over medium-high heat.

2. Season the pork chops on both sides with salt and pepper, to taste.

3. Add the pork chops to the skillet and sear them for about 4 minutes (if boneless) or 5 minutes (if bone-in) on each side, or until they've turned golden.

4. The pork chops will not be done, but remove them from the skillet and place them on a plate.

5. Quickly add the sliced mushrooms to the hot skillet and sauté them with the garlic and thyme, if you are using them. Cook the mushrooms for about 2 minutes, stirring them constantly.

6. Reduce the heat to medium-low and add the heavy cream. Allow the sauce to simmer for 2 to 3 minutes, or until it begins to thicken.

7. Adjust the seasoning in the sauce and place the pork chops back into the pan with the sauce.

8. Cover the skillet and let the pork chops cook for 4 to 5 minutes, or until they have cooked through.

Macros per serving (made with white mushrooms and optional ingredients): 398 calories, 1.1 g net carbs, 1.3 g total carbs, 0.2 g fiber, 0.4 g sugars, 35 g total fat, 19 g protein

Stuffed Portobello Steaks

Makes 4 servings

½ tablespoon extra-virgin olive oil

4 portobello mushroom caps, gills removed (see page 91)

4 ounces cream cheese, softened

½ teaspoon garlic powder

4 slices deli cheese (provolone, Colby, cheddar, Swiss, etc.)

Portobello caps have long been compared with steak, thanks to their thick, meaty texture and savory flavor. Here, they are stuffed with fatty (yummy!) cheese, to create a fun, fast, vegetarian meal. Feel free to add other ingredients (think chopped olives, crumbled bacon, etc.) to complement these steaks.

1. Preheat the oven to 425°F.

2. Massage the olive oil into portobello caps.

3. In a small bowl, mix together the cream cheese and garlic powder.

4. Spoon the cream cheese mixture onto each portobello cap where the gills were removed.

5. Top each stuffed portobello cap with a slice of deli cheese.

6. Place the portobello caps on a baking sheet and cover them loosely with foil, trying to keep the foil off the top of the portobello caps. (You can stick a toothpick in the middle of each stuffed cap, so the foil will rest on the top of the toothpicks, instead of on the melting cheese.)

7. Allow the mushrooms to bake for 20 to 25 minutes, until they're tender and the cheese has melted.

Macros per serving (using provolone cheese): 235 calories, 2.6 g net carbs, 3 g total carbs, 0.4 g fiber, 0.1 g sugars, 19 g total fat, 11 g protein

Stuffed Avocado, Your Way

Makes 2 servings

1 cup cooked Seasoned Ground Beef (see page 40)

4 pickled jalapeño slices, minced

1 teaspoon chile powder

1 large Hass avocado, halved and drizzled with lemon juice to prevent browning

½ cup shredded cheddar cheese

This easy dinner dish isn't a proper recipe as much as it is a blueprint, because you really can fill an avocado with anything you want, from whitefish salad or leftover salmon, to chopped chicken to pulled pork. Here, I use Seasoned Ground Beef (see page 40) and a bit of cheese for garnish.

1. Place the loose meat, minced jalapeño, and chile powder in a skillet over medium heat. Stir the ingredients until they are well combined. You are not recooking the loose meat but simply warming it to "above room temperature" and infusing it with the flavor of the chile powder and jalapeño. Remove the skillet from the heat as soon as the meat is warm to the touch.

2. Spoon the meat mixture into each avocado half and top each with half the shredded cheese.

Macros per serving: 650 calories, 1.3 g net carbs, 8 g total carbs, 6.7 g fiber, 0.7 g sugars, 50 g total fat, 40 g protein

Keto Kielbasa and Cabbage Skillet

Makes 4 servings

2 tablespoons butter

1 small head cabbage, shredded

Salt and pepper, to taste

1 teaspoon onion powder

1 pound kielbasa smoked sausage links, cut into ¼-inch slices

This quick, easy-to-make skillet meal is comforting, full of healthy fiber, and keto compliant. Feel free to use shredded kale instead of cabbage or another type of sausage if you'd like to play with the recipe a bit.

1. Place the butter in a large skillet over medium-high heat.

2. When the butter has melted in the skillet, add the cabbage, salt and pepper, and onion powder. Stir the mixture occasionally and cook just until the cabbage begins to lose its crunch, between 3 and 5 minutes.

3. Add the sliced kielbasa to the cabbage and cover the pan. Cook the mixture for 2 minutes, or until the kielbasa has warmed through and the cabbage is tender.

Macros per serving: 550 calories, 4.5 g net carbs, 10 g total carbs, 5.5 g fiber, 4 g sugars, 40 g total fat, 41 g protein

Keto Pasta Bolognese

Makes 4 servings

1 pound bulk Italian sausage (sweet or hot) or a mix of Italian sausage and ground beef

1 or 2 garlic cloves, minced

½ cup tomato puree

½ cup grated Parmesan cheese

1 (2-pound) spaghetti squash, cut in half and roasted or steamed, spaghetti-like flesh removed

OPTIONAL

1 tablespoon dried oregano

½ tablespoon dried basil

Pinch of crushed red pepper flakes

Salt and pepper, to taste

For this meaty pasta recipe, I use spaghetti squash, for its stringy pastalike consistency. Yet, unlike pasta, spaghetti squash is gluten-free and great for keto eaters. You can also use any type of spiralized vegetable for this recipe.

1. Place a large skillet over medium-high heat and add the meat, garlic, and optional spices. Cook the meat until it is browned and no longer pink. Drain off the fat, if you like.

2. Add the tomato puree and Parmesan cheese to the skillet and allow the mixture to cook until it has thickened, about 10 minutes.

3. Arrange the spaghetti squash on a platter, or on 4 dinner plates, and top with the meat sauce.

Macros per serving (made with sweet Italian sausage and optional ingredients): 524 calories, 7 g net carbs, 12 g total carbs, 5 g fiber, 2 g sugars, 37 g total fat, 31 g protein

Metric Conversion Chart

The recipes that appear in this cookbook use the standard United States method for measuring liquid and dry or solid ingredients (teaspoons, tablespoons, and cups). The information in these charts is provided to help cooks outside the US successfully use these recipes. All equivalents are approximate.

Metric Equivalents for Different Types of Ingredients

STANDARD CUP	FINE POWDER (e.g., flour)	GRAIN (e.g., rice)	GRANULAR (e.g., sugar)	LIQUID SOLIDS (e.g., butter)	LIQUID (e.g., milk)
¾	105 g	113 g	143 g	150 g	180 ml
⅔	93 g	100 g	125 g	133 g	160 ml
½	70 g	75 g	95 g	100 g	120 ml
⅓	47 g	50 g	63 g	67 g	80 ml
¼	35 g	38 g	48 g	50 g	60 ml
⅛	18 g	19 g	24 g	25 g	30 ml

¼ tsp	=				1 ml
½ tsp	=				2 ml
1 tsp	=				5 ml
3 tsp	= 1 tbsp	=	½ fl oz	=	15 ml
	2 tbsp	= ⅛ cup	= 1 fl oz	=	30 ml
	4 tbsp	= ¼ cup	= 2 fl oz	=	60 ml
	5⅓ tbsp	= ⅓ cup	= 3 fl oz	=	80 ml
	8 tbsp	= ½ cup	= 4 fl oz	=	120 ml
	10⅔ tbsp	= ⅔ cup	= 5 fl oz	=	160 ml
	12 tbsp	= ¾ cup	= 6 fl oz	=	180 ml
	16 tbsp	= 1 cup	= 8 fl oz	=	240 ml
	1 pt	= 2 cups	= 16 fl oz	=	480 ml
	1 qt	= 4 cups	= 32 fl oz	=	960 ml
			33 fl oz	=	1000 ml = 1 L

Useful Equivalents for Dry Ingredients by Weight

(To convert ounces to grams, multiply the number of ounces by 30.)

1 oz	=	¹⁄₁₆ lb	=	30 g
2 oz	=	¼ lb	=	120 g
4 oz	=	½ lb	=	240 g
8 oz	=	¾ lb	=	360 g
16 oz	=	1 lb	=	480 g

Useful Equivalents Length

(To convert inches to centimeters, multiply the number of inches by 2.5.)

1 in	=		2.5 cm	
6 in	= ½ ft	=	15 cm	
12 in	= 1 ft	=	30 cm	
36 in	= 3 ft	= 1 yd	= 90 cm	
40 in	=		100 cm	= 1 m

Useful Equivalents for Cooking/Oven Temperatures

	Fahrenheit	Celsius	Gas Mark
Freeze Water	32°F	0°C	
Room Temperature	68°F	20°C	
Boil Water	212°F	100°C	
Bake	325°F	160°C	3
	350°F	180°C	4
	375°F	190°C	5
	400°F	200°C	6
	425°F	220°C	7
	450°F	230°C	8
Broil			Grill

FAQs

It's natural to have questions about ketogenic cooking and eating. Here are some of the most commonly-asked questions about keto meals—with answers to help make ketogenic living easier.

Q I've heard I should stay away from caffeine while on the keto diet, but I notice you include coffee drinks and tea drinks in *The 5-Ingredient Keto Cookbook*.

A There are a lot of conflicting ideas about caffeine and the ketogenic diet. On the one hand, there is evidence that caffeine could disrupt the metabolism of glucose, which could actually knock you out of ketosis, according the American Diabetes Association's magazine, *Diabetes Care*.

On the other hand, there is evidence that drinking a cup or two of coffee (without flavored syrup, caramel, or chocolate shavings) doesn't change things one way or the other on the keto diet—or that it slightly speeds up the metabolism for faster fat burning. In a recent study published in *Canadian Journal of Physiology and Pharmacology*, Canadian researchers evaluated the effects of caffeine consumption in a group of 10 volunteers.

After fasting for 12 hours and then eating breakfast, these individuals were given either no caffeine, the caffeine equivalent of about 1½ cups of coffee, or a caffeine equivalent of 3 cups of coffee. Higher dosages of caffeine in the 10 healthy adults dramatically increased beta-hydroxybutyrate—one of the most studied ketones—in urine. This is a good thing, because the presence of ketones in the urine is an indicator that the body is using fats rather than carbohydrates for energy. This is exactly what you want as a keto eater.

As with so many things, it's up to you to assess for yourself whether or not caffeine supports or prevents ketosis. If you find it difficult to reach or maintain ketosis, try switching things up and either drop or add caffeine to your daily diet. There are caffeinated and caffeine-free recipes in this book, so either way, you're covered!

Q Can I swap low-fat versions of coconut or dairy milk (or cheese or any other high-fat ingredient) for the ingredients called for in keto recipes?

A If you want to stay keto compliant, the answer is no, you cannot. As a keto eater, you need to consume a specific range of fat grams each day to reach, and stay in, ketosis and to give your brain and body the fuel it needs. But you are always allowed to swap ingredients for lower-fat or higher-carb, less expensive, or easier-to-find ingredients. The recipe will, most likely, not be keto compliant if you switch ingredients, but you are always welcome to change things up!

Q Is it okay to substitute ingredients in keto recipes?

A Sometimes. That said, if there is a keto-compliant alternate ingredient for anything in one of the recipes in *The 5-Ingredient Keto Cookbook*, I do mention it. But if you want to keep the recipe keto, most of the time substituting is a no-no. Let's say a recipe calls for a low-carb veggie, such as cucumber, and you want to swap in a red pepper. A traditional recipe wouldn't be affected. A keto, recipe, however, can easily go from low-carb to super-high-carb with just this change.

Q I hear people talk about "dirty keto." What does that mean?

A Isn't this a funny term? Like "plain old keto" (also known in some circles as "original keto"), dirty keto is just as concerned about your macros as regular keto: You get 60 to 75 percent of your diet from fat, 15 to 30 percent from protein, and the remaining 5 to 10 percent from carbs. So far so good, right? Here's where things get interesting: In regular keto, eaters are encouraged to get their macros from whole food sources, like avocado, coconut, beef, salmon, full-fat yogurt, and so on. This means a lot of shopping and meal making or a lot of premade keto meals. In dirty keto, eaters are allowed to use fast food and processed food to reach their macros. So, pork rinds, fast food burgers (without the buns), hot dogs, etc. are acceptable, as long as they are within your macros.

Q Keto eating is so expensive! How do you keep prices down?

A There's a one-word answer to that question: sales. When you see a sale on the keto-approved ingredients you love, stock up so you have them on hand. If you have to, freeze a few salmon steaks or avocados (peel and pit them first, rub them with oil, and then wrap the flesh in freezer wrap). It also helps enormously to make your own lunch the night before. As you clean up after dinner, portion leftovers into containers that you can carry to work or school for lunch the next day.

Q I find cooking in general to be exhausting. Why can't I just order premade keto meals and stock my fridge with frozen keto-compliant grocery meals?

A You can do anything you like, including ordering premade keto meals and purchasing frozen meals. As long as they are made from healthy ingredients and are keto compliant, you'll be fine. However, relying on convenience food can be expensive. It also puts you at the mercy of someone else's taste—their preferred ingredients. Making your own food not only saves you money but you can use your favorite ingredients, while avoiding the ones you either don't like or that don't agree with you.

My advice: Learn a few recipes from this book and you'll always have something to eat. I like to spend a couple hours over the weekend making a few meals ahead of time, so during a busy week I can truly just grab and go.

Another tip: If you have keto-eating friends or coworkers, double or triple your recipes, divide them into single-serve containers, and share them. Ask that your friends or coworkers do the same. This easy "cooking co-op" saves huge amounts of time and is a fun way to ensure that everyone sticks to the eating plan.

Q There are traditional recipes that I love. Is there a way to "keto-ize" them?

A Yes, although there is a very good chance that after those recipes have been "keto-ized," they will look nothing like the food you love so much. There is a plethora of cookbooks and websites that are dedicated to keto-izing traditional recipes. Typically, any carbohydrate-heavy ingredient (such as grains, potatoes, pasta, and the like) is swapped for a low-carb vegetable substitute (zucchini, anyone?) or completely removed. I personally find it is easier to stick to recipes that were designed especially for keto eating, rather than trying to overhaul carbohydrate-heavy mainstream meals. But I do encourage you to explore all your keto-compliant options to come up with meals you love to eat—and prepare.

Q Purchased keto snacks . . . do they exist?

A Yes, they do. In fact, according to the market trend company Market Analysists Global, the keto product market was USD 1,078,300 million in 2014 and USD 1,221,500 in 2017. The global keto diet market size will grow by USD 1.11 billion by 2023, according to marketing trends company Technavio's report *Global Keto Diet Market 2019–2023*. While there is no breakdown of the share of those numbers that went to keto snack items and the share that went to other keto products (such as prepared meals), all it takes is a walk through your local grocery store to see how many keto snacks are available at mainstream retailers. Bars, chips, jerky, cookies, meat sticks, popsicles, ice cream, and more, are all available in keto versions.

Q My family eats dinner together each night. Is it safe for everyone to be eating the keto food I make? Or do I need to make a separate meal for my spouse and kids?

A Personally, I would prepare a separate meal for your spouse and kids. I bet that is not what you wanted to hear! The ketogenic diet is not for everyone, and if your partner has a diagnosed (or undiagnosed) health condition, daily ketogenic meals could worsen his or her condition. Further, children need a larger share of carbohydrates for their growing bodies to use as fuel for growth and energy. Their growing bodies also need the antioxidants and phytonutrients that come with vegetables and fruit.

I understand if this is not the answer you wanted to hear. Making two dinners (or lunches or breakfasts) is time consuming, and it doesn't seem fair to have to make a meal that you are not going to eat. If it helps make your life easier, I'll share the time-saving way I handle this in my own home: I make a keto-compliant green salad (which typically is based on baby spinach leaves) and portion off a serving for myself, to which I add all manner of keto ingredients (crumbled bacon, diced avocado, etc.). Or I'll make spiralized zucchini, which I eat with butter and a side serving of whatever protein (salmon, pork loin, lamb chops) we are eating. I stop with that, but everyone else gets marinara sauce on their spiralized zucchini, as well as a side serving of a superfood grain (like quinoa or amaranth), which I have made in bulk on my "cook day" (Sunday), and a small serving of fruit. In this way, we all share a few components of the meal, but I stick to keto-compliant foods, and everyone else gets a few different or additional items.

Q Can I add extra fat to my portion of family meals and call it "keto"?

A Not usually. If you are eating a more traditional-style, mainstream meal, adding extra fat to it may help you meet your daily requirement of fat grams, but you'll most likely take in too many carbohydrates and perhaps even too much protein to maintain your keto diet. That's why ketogenic eating can be so challenging: You not only have to eat a large amount of fat, you also have to greatly limit your carbohydrates as well as your protein intake, albeit to a lesser degree.

Q How do I handle dinner parties and holiday meals as a keto eater?

A Eat before you arrive and tell yourself you are there to talk to everyone you can! Grab a glass of seltzer the moment you walk in the door—this keeps you slightly occupied so you're less likely to pick at any of the nibbles that may be stationed about—and move as far away from the food table as you can. Never eat casseroles, any type of baked good, anything that looks or tastes sweet, and stay away from the alcohol because it lowers your resistance to dinner rolls, lasagna, and pumpkin pie. Think about bringing a keto-safe dish or two. And put on your plate only those things you know are

keto compliant. Be so busy speaking with everyone that the host can't interrupt to urge you to try the risotto. In other words, don't arrive hungry and find things other than food to occupy yourself!

Q How do I handle dinner parties and holiday meals as a keto cook?

A Make the meal keto, including a few vegan keto items for those of your friends who eat only plant foods. If making all that food seems like too much work, purchase prepared dishes. If you want to put out a few platters of not-keto-safe foods, make sure they are things that you do not enjoy, so you won't be tempted to nibble at them.

Q I despise eggs. Can I still eat and cook keto?

A Eggs really do seem to be the keto "poster child," don't they? I dislike eggs, too, actually, and do fine eating keto. For breakfast, there are all kinds of non-egg, keto-compliant things you can enjoy, including a smoothie, full-fat Greek yogurt, and bacon or sausage. Check out other breakfast recipes in chapter 4. Another, perhaps even easier, option is to enjoy leftovers from last night's dinner. (That's what I do!) I firmly believe that to succeed at a diet (regardless of what it is), you need to enjoy the food you are eating.

Q I notice you have "mocktail" recipes in this book, but no cocktail recipes. Should I be avoiding alcohol while on the keto diet?

A Alcohol is fun. At least I think it is. I really enjoy a glass of red wine with my husband after work; a beer at a game; a goblet of sangria at my favorite Spanish restaurant. I like it all. But I am going to be honest: After one drink I am more likely to eat something that is not keto. You may have more willpower than I do, but I guarantee that after downing two or three drinks, you'll be more tempted to mindlessly stuff your face with a stray carb than you would if you hadn't had a drink at all. And just like that, you've thrown yourself out of ketosis. This is perhaps the least-discussed danger of drinking on a keto diet—and it's the reason I tell people to take a break from drinking while they're on the ketogenic plan.

Then there is the way that a keto-fed body metabolizes alcohol. When you're in ketosis, your body uses your stored fat for energy. When you add alcohol to your body, your liver will default to using the byproducts of the metabolized alcohol instead of the fat you want it to use.

Having said that, there are a few alcoholic options that are safer than others—as long as you have no more than one drink at a time and limit yourself to no more than one drink per week. Look for clear or amber liquors that are around 40 percent alcohol by volume (vodka, whiskey, gin, scotch, brandy, rum, and tequila). These generally contain 0 carbs and sugars on their own. Just make sure to drink them neat, on the rocks, or mixed with straight water or seltzer. Anything else is going to add carbs to the mix.

One last thing about drinking while eating keto: You'll get drunk more easily. Carbs slow down the metabolization of alcohol, so it takes longer for you to feel the effect of what you drink. Without dietary carbs, the effects of alcohol occur quickly. Be prepared!

Q I feel so thirsty on the ketogenic diet. I have heard that it's common to be a bit dehydrated while eating keto. Why? And what can I do about it?

A Hydration is a topic of much discussion in keto communities, probably because dehydration is one of the first symptoms you may notice when you go keto. There are several reasons for this. If you've ever tried a low-carb diet before, you may have noticed a large amount of weight loss in the first week. It isn't uncommon to lose up to 10 pounds during the first week of a keto diet. You've probably also noticed how often you find yourself in the bathroom. That's because your body is no longer using glycogen (stored carbs) for fuel.

As your body's stash of these carbs dwindles and it begins to use fat instead for fuel, something interesting happens. You begin to lose large amounts of water. That's because each gram of glycogen that is stored in the body helps the body hold on to 3 to 4 grams of water in the form of "water weight." As the glycogen stores dwindle, so does the stored water trapped in your body—most of which is lost through urination—but you lose a lot through respiration, as well. Staying hydrated by drinking at least 1 liter of water a day helps ensure that you feel good and your body systems work efficiently. This water will not be stored: You'll excrete it along with any stored water. The result of so much excreted water can be a loss of electrolytes, minerals that play a crucial role in keeping the body hydrated and supporting nerve and muscle function.

One of the easiest ways to replace electrolytes is an electrolyte drink. You may be familiar with some of the mainstream options, which are available, typically, in garish neon greens, reds, oranges, yellows, and blues—and are sold in large plastic bottles. These drinks are filled with a range of minerals that your body needs to replace after heavy sweating (or vomiting). For a keto eater, these drinks present a problem: They are loaded with carbs. There are special keto-created electrolyte drinks on the market, however, but they are expensive and difficult to find. An economical, convenient option is to make your own electrolyte drink. Here are two easy recipes: Salty Keto Water and Electrolyte Sipper, both on page 69.

Q I notice the only sweetener used in *The 5-Ingredient Keto Cookbook* is stevia. Is it okay to use honey, molasses, or maple syrup instead?

A Unfortunately, no. Not if you want to reach, and stay in, ketosis. Most sweeteners (even natural ones) are loaded with carbohydrates. This is why most keto recipes rely on stevia, which is close to carb free. To get an idea of the net carb counts in a range of sweeteners, you can refer to this list:

The High Carb Price of Sweeteners

SWEETENER	SERVING SIZE	AVERAGE NET CARB COUNT
White table sugar (cane sugar)	1 tablespoon	15 g
Raw cane sugar (turbinado sugar)	1 tablespoon	12 g
Brown sugar, loosely packed	1 tablespoon	8.76 g
Molasses	1 tablespoon	15 g
Honey	1 tablespoon	17.3 g
Agave nectar	1 tablespoon	12 g
Maple syrup (pure)	1 tablespoon	13.42 g
Corn syrup	1 tablespoon	15.36 g
Barley malt syrup	1 tablespoon	17.11 g
Brown rice syrup	8 drops	18 g
Liquid stevia	1 teaspoon	0 g
Powdered stevia	1 teaspoon	0.5 g

Keto Resources

Many wonderful resources are available to the new keto eater. Here are some of my favorites:

Books and Cookbooks

The Complete Book of Food Counts, 9th Edition: The Book That Counts It All (Dell), by Corinne T. Netzer. In this day of online searching, do you really need a book of food counts? Maybe not, but having a book you can quickly open to find the macros (and micros, too, if you'd like) of any ingredient is helpful.

Good Housekeeping Keto Diet (Sterling), by the editors of Good Housekeeping. From a trusted name in American homemaking comes a keto cookbook that features just what you'd expect: homey, comforting traditional foods with a keto-compliant twist.

The Keto Kit (Sterling Publishing), by Stephanie Pedersen, is available at Barnes and Noble stores and at B&N online. This three-book-set was designed for new keto eaters, and features a book about the science of ketogenic eating, a cookbook of 100+ fun keto recipes, and a journal to record things that affect your ability to get into ketosis and lose weight (hydration, sleep, stress, exercise, to name a few).

Living Low Carb: Revised & Updated Edition (Sterling), by Jonny Bowden, Barry Sears, and Will Cole, takes a deep dive into the world of carbohydrates and how to live with fewer of them. Useful for all keto eaters!

The Art and Science of Low Carbohydrate Living: An Expert Guide to Making the Life-Saving Benefits of Carbohydrate Restriction Sustainable and Enjoyable (Beyond Obesity), by Jeff Volek and Stephen Phinney. Delve into the medical and health uses of low-carb diets for a better understanding of how low-carb diets (such as the ketogenic diet) work.

The Ketogenic Bible: The Authoritative Guide to Ketosis (Victory Belt), by Jacob Wilson and Ryan Lowrey. Research, research, and more research, this is the definitive tome on all things keto, from its beginnings as a treatment for epilepsy through decades of research to its current use as a weight-loss diet.

Keto Lifestyle

http://happyketo.com/ Would you like a recipe for keto carrot cake with cream cheese frosting? Or Japanese Ajitsuke Tamago (aka keto ramen eggs)? Maybe you'd like to learn more about keto eating in Japan? Or study lists of keto-compliant ingredients? This beautiful, unusual site is for you!

https://www.heyketomama.com This easy-to-read blog is written by a keto-eating mom who loves to bake. You'll find recipes for such tempting treats as Keto Strawberry Donuts and Keto Fudge. If you're a fan of online shopping, you'll find lists of promo codes for various keto-friendly online stores.

https://hip2keto.com Hip2Keto has helpful articles on a wide array of keto issues, from maintaining ketosis to dining out. There are also "keto finds" and "keto deals" sections.

https://www.ketoconnect.net/ This fun site is like sitting down with your smart best friend. Full of wonderful advice here on how to "live keto." You'll also find meal plans, recipes (including a "keto version of your favorite recipe" section), and online classes.

https://meatfreeketo.com/ If you've eaten keto for any length of time, you know how plant-starved you become after a few days. Meat Free Keto addresses that, by giving you resources, advice, and recipes to eat vegan while remaining keto-compliant.

https://nobunplease.com/ No Buns Please is a fun site that offers up a generous helping of keto resources (including how to eat keto at a number of national chain restaurants), and keto recipes for yummy dishes such as Broccoli & Cheese Keto Waffles and Keto Fauxtatoes.

https://www.ruled.me/start-here/ RuledMe is a popular website that offers a soup-to-nuts lineup of keto-oriented topics, from how to begin, to the "keto calculator" that helps you come up with the number of macros you may want to eat each day to meet your goals.

Keto Shopping

https://www.amazon.com/ If you're having difficulty locating keto-compliant ingredients or kitchen tools that can make the keto diet easier, online shopping can be a diet-saver. Amazon carries everything you may need to succeed on your keto diet, from lunch bags to coconut oil in bulk to digital food scales to keto-safe snacks.

https://www.factor75.com/ Unlike many keto meal services that deliver meals frozen, Factor 75 sends fresh meals anywhere in the contiguous United States. Be sure to specify "keto" when ordering; the service also makes paleo meals.

https://ketoand.co/ Keto & Co features a range of packaged keto foods, including dehydrated riced cauliflower, keto brownie mix, keto flat bread mix, stevia, glycerin, and more.

https://www.ketofridge.com/ Keto Fridge is a nationwide keto meal service that brings premade keto meals right to your door.

https://ketohc.com Keto Health Care sells fat calipers, digital sales, breath meters, and various supplements.

https://www.territoryfoods.com/ Territory Foods delivers prepared keto meals that you just heat and eat. **Note**: As of printing time, Territory Foods delivers only to selected cities in California, Texas, Virginia, Maryland, Washington, DC, Pennsylvania, and New York. Plans are in the works to roll out nationwide delivery.

https://www.kissmyketo.com Kiss My Keto is an online keto store that sells keto urine test strips. There is also an informative blog with first person guest posts from a variety of keto experts.

https://www.netrition.com Netrition is an online supplement seller that has a large "keto section" with packaged goods, keto-targeted supplements, hydration products, powders, and more, that can make your ketogenic journey easier.

https://thrivemarket.com/keto Thrive Market is an online market that sells snacks, premade food, supplies, and even self-care items according to what diet you follow (options include paleo, vegan, and of course, keto).

Health and Diet Resources

https://charliefoundation.org Charlie Abraham saw a disappearance of epilepsy symptoms when he tried a keto diet. His website dives deep into the large number of health conditions that have been shown by research to be improved by a keto diet.

https://www.ditchthecarbs.com/ Ditch the Carbs is not dedicated to keto eating, but it can help you navigate the ketogenic diet by helping you understand how carbs work, what they are, which foods contain them, and how to remove them from your diet.

https://ketogasm.com/ Though KetoGasm has a blog, the big draw is the information. It has a wealth of detailed info on every part of the keto diet, from acceptable alcoholic beverages to the ins and outs of ketosis.

https://www.ketogenic-diet-resource.com/ This comprehensive website not only talks about how the keto diet works, but takes a look at the various health conditions that may be helped by the diet. It also includes a list of resources.

https://www.nutritionadvance.com/ An easy-to-navigate site with a wide range of helpful articles on low-carb diets.

https://www.verywellfit.com/recipe-nutrition-analyzer-4157076 VeryWellFit's recipe nutrition analyzer is a brilliant tool to help calculate the macros in your favorite recipes. Just plug in the ingredients and the number of servings a recipe makes, and you'll have a custom-generated list of macros.

Acknowledgments

I want to acknowledge you, dear reader, the very person *The 5-Ingredient Keto Cookbook* was created for. Keto eating is a wonderful, change-creating journey to managing your weight, reducing inflammation, getting rid of cravings, supporting brain health, and more. As powerful as the ketogenic diet is, however, it's no secret that this high-fat, low-carb eating plan can be a bit complicated. But I am assuming that since you are here, you are in the middle of creating a healthier way of being for yourself. Congratulations! I am here to support you by making keto meals easier.

Instead of recipes with long, expensive ingredient lists and complicated instructions, *The 5-Ingredient Keto Cookbook* was designed to simplify your high-fat meal prep, so you have time for all the other wonderful people, places, activities, and things that you'd like to turn your attention to.

For me, that means my family, who I am going to thank here! Hubby Richard Demler, thank you for being a rock. You do what you do, so the rest of us can do what we do. Thank you. To my oldest son, Leif Christian Pedersen, you continually amaze me with your deep insight, your humor, your curiosity (which is my favorite of all human qualities), your handsomeness, your sartorial smarts, your intelligence, and that great big voice of yours. To my middle son, Anders Gyldenvalde Pedersen. Your poise, your humanity, your stunningness (is that a word?), your curiosity (yes, you have it too!),

your intellect, your unusual take on the world, your gorgeous voice—you are one fantastic kid. And to you, Axel SuneLund Pedersen. You, Mr. Smarty, are so lucky to have that exquisite brain of yours and that adorable sense of humor and the ability to talk to, and connect with, anyone and everyone—and yes, I love your curiosity, as well. Thanks to all of you for looking out for one another, and for looking out for me while I wrote *The 5-Ingredient Keto Cookbook*. May you boys use your gifts for good.

Thank you, too, to my wonderful editor, Jennifer Williams. It was a delight working with you again. Thanks, too, to our copy editor, Melanie Gold, who ensured that my recipes were accurate, my prose clean, and my grammar correct, and to our project editor, Hannah Reich, whose efficiency and talent ensured that this book arrived at its publishing destination right on time. Finally, *The 5-Ingredient Keto Cookbook* owes its beautiful photos to food photographer Bill Milne, and its sleek, modern, oh-so-attractive look to the art department at Sterling Publishing.

Thank you so much, everyone, for your role in bringing *The 5-Ingredient Keto Cookbook* to being. I hope you like it! It was made with you in mind!

Thank you, thank you, thank you!

Happy keto to you!

Much love,

Stephanie

Index

(continued on following page)

(continued on following page)

About the Author

STEPHANIE PEDERSEN, CHHC, AADP, is a nutrition educator, cookbook author, and media host. Author of more than twenty books, Stephanie knows what it feels like to juggle a busy schedule with the desire to be healthy. "As a mother, writer, stage mom, and someone who loves to have time alone to wander local farmers' markets, I know that complicated, overly fussy diets, or an unnatural obsession with calorie counting, are not the answers to getting and staying healthy." Instead, Stephanie espouses a life of love, laughter, daily exercise, and your favorite whole foods.

   As Stephanie says, "I want health for everyone! I have seen firsthand with myself and my own clients that when one works to get clean and fit and address one's health challenges, life gets bigger. Suddenly, life becomes outrageously fun and easy. You move healthfully through life with ease."

You can find Stephanie online at www.StephaniePedersen.com, where you can read more about how she creates her own brand of healthy living. You'll find recipes, photos, tutorials, strategies, and more for creating a sane, productive, comfort-filled life. Stop by and access episodes of Stephanie's podcasts, read chapters of her books, and say hello.

Also by Stephanie Pedersen and Sterling Publishing

American Cozy: Hygge-Inspired Ways
to Create Comfort & Happiness

*

The Keto Kit

*

Roots: The Complete Guide to
the Underground Superfood

*

Berries: The Complete Guide to Cooking
with Power-Packed Berries

*

Coconut: The Complete Guide to the
World's Most Versatile Superfood

*

The 7-Day Superfood Cleanse

*

Kale: The Complete Guide to the
World's Most Powerful Superfood